DATE DUE

ELICITATION EXPERIMENTS IN ENGLISH

Miami Linguistics Series

No. 1. Germanic Studies in Honor of Edward Henry Sehrt
Edited by Frithjof A. Ravent, Wolfram K. Legner, and James C. King

No. 2. A Linguistic Study of the English Verb
By F. R. Palmer

No. 3. Multilingual Lexicon of Linguistics and Philology:
English, Russian, German, French
By Rose Nash

No. 4. Studies in Spanish Phonology
By Tomás Navarro

No. 5. Studies in English Adverbial Usage
By Sidney Greenbaum

No. 6. General Characteristics of the Germanic Languages
By Antoine Meillet

No. 7. Language: Its Structure and Evolution
By Marcel Cohen

No. 8. Problems of General Linguistics
By Emile Benveniste

No. 9. Linguistic Variability and Intellectual Development
By Wilhelm von Humboldt

Miami Linguistics Series No. 10

Elicitation Experiments in English

Linguistic Studies in Use and Attitude

Sidney Greenbaum
Associate Professor of English
University of Wisconsin-Milwaukee

Randolph Quirk
Quain Professor of English Language and Literature
University of London

UNIVERSITY OF MIAMI PRESS
Coral Gables, Florida

Preface

The experimental work underlying the present study was conducted within the Survey of English Usage and we are grateful for the ready co-operation of Survey colleagues, past and present. Our chief debt is to Jan Svartvik, who has given freely of his time and unique experience throughout: ideas on design, help in administering batteries, and detailed critical comments on a first draft of this book. Caroline Bott has been responsible for all the analyses of a statistical nature and for the programs by which the results of Batteries III and IIIa were computed. On the computational side more generally, we are happy to express our gratitude also to the staff of the Computer Centre of University College London; to Gordon Robbie of Her Majesty's Stationery Office; and to Ruth Kempson, who helped in this as well as in other respects. Valerie Adams, Margot Charlton, Derek Davy, Norman Fairclough, and Joan Huddleston also provided valuable help at various stages of the work, and in connexion with Battery IV we are glad to acknowledge the help also of Hannah Steinberg. The work was financially supported in part from a grant to the Survey of English Usage by HM Department of Education and Science and by a research grant for the summer of 1969 from the University of Wisconsin-Milwaukee. Finally, we are grateful to Peggy Drinkwater for her skill and friendly help in guiding the book through the press.

S G
R Q

February 1970

Contents

Preface   v

Figures   ix

Tables   xi

1 The aims of elicitation experiments   1

2 Experimental design   8

3 The relevant aspects of responses   19

4 Testing the test design   26

5 Comparability and consistency   37

6 The influence of experimental environment   50

7 Linguistic problems and scoring criteria   59

8 Linguistic problems and experimental variation   67

9 Use and attitude: the relation between test results   81

10 Conclusion   113

Tabular appendices   119

Bibliographical references   153

Figures

1   *Use and attitude*   1

2   *Types of test*   3

3   *Specimen preference test*   16

4   *Scoring system*   19

5   *Test and group variability*   41

6   *Consistency of individuals*   44

7   *Consistency of individuals*   46

8   *Consistency of individuals*   47

9   *Consistency of individuals*   48

10 *Attitudes to experiment*   51

11 *Attitudes to experiment*   56

12a *Compliance and evaluation scores: category order*   84

12b *Compliance and evaluation scores: category order*   85

13 *The relation of Figs 12 to Figs 14*   87

14a *Compliance and evaluation scores: result profiles*   88

14b *Compliance and evaluation scores: result profiles*   89

14c *Compliance and evaluation scores: result profiles*   90

14d *Compliance and evaluation scores: result profiles*   91

15 *Similarity and evaluation scores: result profiles*   104

16 *Selection and preference scores: result profiles*   108

Tables

1 *Compliance tests: Battery I*   120

2 *Compliance tests: Battery II*   122

3 *Compliance tests: Battery III*   124

4 *Compliance tests: Battery IIIa*   126

5 *Selection tests: Battery II*   128

6 *Selection tests: Battery III*   128

7 *Selection tests: Battery IIIa*   129

8 *Evaluation tests: Battery I*   129

9 *Evaluation tests: Battery II*   132

10 *Evaluation tests: Battery III*   134

11 *Similarity tests: Battery I*   135

12 *Similarity tests: Battery II*   137

13 *Similarity tests: Battery III*   138

14 *Preference tests: Battery III*   139

15 *Compliance tests: Battery IV*   140

16 *Evaluation tests: Battery IV*   141

17 *Group results - Compliance and evaluation tests: Battery II*   143

18 *Group results - Compliance and evaluation tests: Battery III*   146

19 *Group results - Similarity tests: Battery II*   148

20 *Group results - Similarity tests: Battery III*   148

21 *Group results - Selection tests: Battery II*   149

22 *Group results - Selection tests: Battery III*   149

23 *Group results - Preference tests: Battery III*   151

Chapter 1

The aims of
elicitation experiments

The central concern of this book is the pursuit of experimental methods whereby grammatical and semantic inquiry can be put on a satisfying objective basis. It is true, but misleadingly curt, to say that our aims are to find out whether a given form is acceptable. Not merely is it misleading in as much as it implies a 'yes or no' decision: it is misleading also in implying that 'acceptability' is a simple, unified phenomenon. The techniques explored in this monograph are designed to cope with a multifaceted acceptability within which it is essential as a minimum to make the distinctions displayed in *Fig* 1.

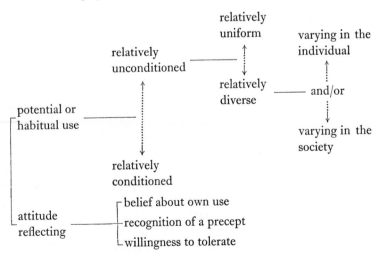

Fig 1: Use and attitude

It will be noted that 'actual' use is not mentioned in the figure; indeed, the purpose of our experiments is to move beyond the instances of actual usage (as recorded in a corpus) to the material for which elicitation techniques are required. But even so, we need a distinction between 'potential' and 'habitual' for material so elicited. That is to say, we must postulate the case in which the elicited sentence embodies essential features which a subject has encountered before (the past of *learn* or the occurrence of *hardly* between auxiliary and nonfinite verb, for example); this is what we understand by 'habitual'. But equally we must postulate the case in which the elicited sentence has an essential feature which a subject may never have been called upon to use but which is in some sense 'available' to him (within his 'competence', to change the metalanguage); this is what we understand by 'potential'. For example, we may wonder what a subject would supply as the past of a strange verb such as /flaiv/ or the way in which he would position the adverb *introductorily* or indeed (*cf* Jacobson 1964, 238) *blondely*. This is far from suggesting, however, that instances can be unambiguously tagged as 'habitual' or 'potential'.

A word or two may be added in explanation of some other distinctions made in *Fig* 1. The pair 'conditioned' and 'unconditioned' should be seen as polar terms on a graded scale, and the former should be read as 'conditioned by specifiable linguistic or situational factors'. A similar scale is of course indicated by 'relatively uniform' and 'relatively diverse', the latter pole being often referred to as 'free variation', a term avoided here because of its doubtful implications: one may question whether diversity is ever entirely unconditioned. Such variation may be a property of the individual, as when a Mr X vacillates between /saiˈkɔlədʒi/ and /psaiˈkɔlədʒi/ in his pronunciation without this reflecting a similar vacillation in society as a whole. Equally, society as a whole may show variation between /iːðə/ and /aiðə/ without this being reflected in the pronunciation of Mr Y, who says only /aiðə/. But these are not of course mutually exclusive and indeed it may be supposed that a variation in society usually corresponds to a comparable variation in the individuals who comprise that society.

If elicited behaviour is different from the 'actual' behaviour casually observed and (if one is lucky) collected in a corpus, it is at least equally important to distinguish elicited usage from attitudes to usage. And these attitudes can be seen as reflecting three potentially quite distinct but often interacting factors. We may have strong beliefs about the forms we habitually use and we may also have strong views about the forms that ought to be used; these may be in harmony or in rueful conflict, but –

needless to say – our beliefs about our own usage in no way necessarily correspond to the facts of our actual usage. Furthermore, we may tolerate usage in others that corresponds neither to the forms we believe we use ourselves nor to the forms that we believe are the most to be commended.

The discussion of our aims will be simplified if we outline at this point the experimental structure within which our inquiries have taken place. In *Fig* 2 we display the types of test and the relation between them. It is important to emphasise the basic division between performance tests and judgment tests, since from each subject and on each problem we normally elicit responses in two complementary tests, a Performance test (our chief method of eliciting a subject's *use*) and a Judgment test (our chief method of eliciting his *attitude*).

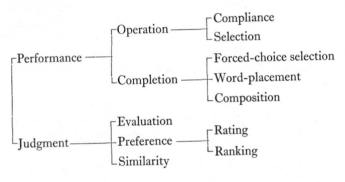

Fig 2: Types of test

Performance tests comprise operation tests and completion tests, differentiated according to the type of tasks required of subjects. For operation tests, subjects are asked to effect some change in a given sentence, while for completion tests they are asked to make some addition to a given sentence. Chapter 7 lists the categories of linguistic problem investigated in the operation tests we discuss in this book.

Operation tests comprise compliance and selection tests, which differ in the nature of the linguistic problem they pose. In compliance tests, some deviance is suspected in the sentence presented to subjects or in the sentence resulting from the change they are asked to make, except that some sentences thought to be non-deviant are interpolated as a control and for contrast. For example, subjects were asked to replace *he* by *they* in the sentence *He hardly could sit still*. It was predicted that the position of *hardly* in this sentence would be unacceptable to many subjects.

Indeed, by transposing *hardly* in their responses to the position between auxiliary and verb, the majority of subjects not only pinpointed what they found objectionable in the sentence, but also indicated by their alteration of the sentence what they considered to be the acceptable position of *hardly* in this type of structure. It was therefore not surprising that when these subjects were asked to perform the same task on the sentence *He could hardly sit still*, they retained the adverb in this position. In some compliance tests, however, the deviance emerges only as a result of the task required of the subjects. Thus, subjects were asked to turn into a question the sentence *He will probably stay late*. There is no reason, of course, to think that the sentence given to them was in any way deviant. But the sentence resulting from the application of the task raises the problem of the acceptability of *probably* in the interrogative form of the sentence, the extent of the problem being indicated by the alterations that subjects carry out.

Selection tests are devised as a method for investigating divided usage. They are rather like the last type of compliance test in that the sentence presented to the subjects is not thought to be deviant. However, when subjects perform the specified task, they have to choose (whether or not they are conscious of choosing) between two or more variant forms. For example, subjects were asked to make the verb present in *None of the children answered the question*. The task obliged the subjects to choose between the singular and plural forms of the verb and their responses automatically indicated which form they preferred to use.

Completion tests comprise forced-choice selection tests, word-placement tests, and composition tests. The first of these, like the ordinary selection tests described above, are devised for the study of divided usage. The difference is that subjects are given a limited set of items from which to select and a limited set of environments in which their selected form is to be used. For example, given

I ——————the poem.
I have ——————the poem.

together with the two forms *learned* and *learnt*, we investigate not what is the subject's general preference as between -*ed* and -*t* (as in ordinary selection tests) but his preference for one or other form as preterite or past participle if he is forced to choose. See further Quirk 1970b and Kempson and Quirk 1970.

As the term indicates, word-placement tests are designed to investigate word position. Subjects are given a sentence and a word that they are required to use with it. For example, subjects were asked to use *usually* with *My brother plays the guitar*. By their placement of *usually* they indicated which position in the structure they preferred for this adverb.

Composition tests, unlike the other completion tests, are open-ended. Subjects are given part of a sentence and are told its position in the putative final form of the sentence. They are then instructed to complete the sentence in any way they like. For example, subjects were given *I entirely* as the opening words of the sentence they were required to complete. In this particular instance, we were interested in the verbs which co-occur with these opening words as compared with those co-occurring with, for example, *I completely*. An analysis of the results of composition tests conducted so far as well as a discussion of further uses of this technique will be found in Greenbaum 1970.

Three types of judgment tests have been used: evaluation, preference, and similarity tests. In evaluation tests, normally complementary to compliance tests, subjects are required to evaluate a sentence on a three-point scale: 'perfectly natural and normal', 'wholly unnatural and abnormal' and 'somewhere between'. For example, subjects have been asked to judge in this way the acceptability of a sentence they had been given earlier in a compliance test, *He hardly could sit still*.

Preference tests, on the other hand, are normally complementary to selection tests. They comprise two components, rating and ranking. Subjects are given two or more variant forms of a sentence, for example *None of the children answers the question* and *None of the children answer the question*. They are then required to rate the sentences, using the same three-point scale as in the evaluation test, but this time the juxtaposition of the two forms inevitably focuses evaluative attention on the only variation between them. They are also required to rank the sentences in order of preference.

The similarity test also involves a judgment on the relationship between sentences, but this time it is the semantic relationship that is in question. Subjects are given two sentences, usually with minimal lexical and syntactic differences between them, and are asked to judge their similarity on a three-point scale: 'very similar in meaning', 'very different in meaning', and 'somewhere between'. This judgment was required, for example, on the pair of sentences (given here in a prosodic transcription explained in Crystal and Quirk 1964)

/some lectures are actually given before tèn#
/ăctually# /some lectures are given before tèn#

Similarity tests, including this particular instance, have generally been used as complementary to compliance tests.

Not all these types of test have been used to an equal extent up to the present, and indeed in this book we are concerned chiefly with batteries that have consisted predominantly of *compliance* tests with their corresponding *evaluation* tests. The results in each battery are displayed in the Tabular Appendices.

As already stated, our techniques aim at exploring all these facets of acceptability, but this is not a matter of whether a form is acceptable or not. Acceptability is gradable and we are concerned with the extent to which a sentence is unacceptable. But of course we also want to know the precise point at which it is unacceptable, and in what respect it is unacceptable. The latter, for example, is in important ways deducible from the direction that 'rectification' of a deviant sentence takes at the hands of subjects in a compliance test. More positively, sufficiently varied types of information are sought so that we can establish the normal position of adverbs in declarative and interrogative sentences, the normal process of negation, and such like. For example, with a test sentence *The council lowered his rent slightly* and the requirement that the subjects make the verb present tense, more explicit information on the subjects' normal usage is given by those who move *slightly* than by those who leave it unchanged. Moreover, among those who found it acceptable in the evaluation test there were some who moved the adverb in the compliance test; such a discrepancy illustrates the contrast between an *attitude* of tolerance and a preference in *use*. It is also important to recognise that a preference in use need not correspond to a preference in attitude. For example, with the subject phrase *None of the children*, a singular verb (prescribed by schoolroom precept) was preferred in a judgment test more frequently than it was preferred in a selection test. On the other hand, we need to recognise that there is in general a fairly close harmony between attitude and use, as is shown in Chapter 9. For example, about a third of the subjects gave as their first choice in the preference test *I have smelled the flowers* and about a third also supplied the form *smelled* in the selection test where the same sentence was involved.

In this connexion, we may mention that the preference tests give us an obvious example of the way in which our work can distinguish between variation in the individual and variation in society (*Fig* 1). They show that some subjects can prefer one form while other subjects prefer a different one (variation in society); and they also show that some subjects give an identically high ranking to two or more forms (variation in the individual).

It is hoped that it will now be clear that our scheme of test techniques (*Fig* 2) can be regarded as a promising source of data corresponding to the categories of use and attitude (*Fig* 1). Some of these categories of course respond more satisfactorily and sensitively to experimental inquiry than others, and there can be little doubt that 'habitual behaviour' is the most difficult to ascertain by such means. We do not claim that a simple equation can be made between this and even the most overwhelming results our experiments can elicit. We are well aware that we cannot escape from the artificiality of the test situation, though with continuing refinement we can hope to remove some of the worst effects of bias that the test situation introduces. Meantime, we can be sure that the alternatives are considerably less promising: reliance upon corpus alone and reliance upon introspection alone. Both need supplementation by experimental evidence.

Chapter 2

Experimental design

Our experiments are an extension of the techniques developed in Quirk and Svartvik 1966 (hereafter QS). In QS, a battery consisted of 50 performance and 50 judgment tests, allowing the whole battery to be administered well within a lecture period. We have seen no reason for any general departure from this convenient battery-length. The QS tests were characteristically in pairs which contrasted deviance and non-deviance in respect of a single linguistic feature. As well as such pairs, there were non-deviant sentences where the tester's interest lay in the specific form selected by subjects. As a result, about half the test sentences were non-deviant and this was (and has continued to be) regarded as important in order to avoid the development of an expectation of deviance.

The tests were administered orally by the tester standing in front of a group of subjects, the only control on consistency being the fact that he read from a prepared script which specified the forms of instructions to a prearranged plan and which prosodically specified the way in which the test sentences should be read out. The instructions, which gave no hint that the sentences to be heard would include deviant ones, listed the tasks and gave examples of their performance. The test sentences came at timed intervals, the intervals (of 20 seconds' duration) being measured from the beginning of one test to the beginning of the next. Tasks stipulated for operation tests were as follows (QS 22f): change of tense to present or to past; change to negative or to affirmative; replacement of a subject pronoun by a stated singular or plural form; turning a statement into an 'inversion question' introduced by a specified form of *be* or *do*. These tasks were introduced in a varied order, but 'paired' tests (though always widely separated in the test sequence) required the same task. In blocks of roughly ten, the procedure varied as to whether subjects were told first the task to be performed or the sentence to which a task was to be applied.

Until the instructions for the subsequent judgment tests (in all cases, of the evaluation type), the tester was careful to mask from the subjects the fact that the experiment had anything to do with linguistic acceptability. But at the beginning of these instructions, subjects were told they would hear 'the same sentences again, this time at much shorter intervals', and they were now invited to judge their acceptability on a three-point scale:

Wholly natural and normal
Marginal or dubious
Wholly unnatural and abnormal

For the evaluation component, the sentences read out were the same as the sentences given in the compliance tests (before task performance) and they were presented in the same order. The sentences came at timed intervals (of five seconds' duration), again measured from the beginning of one test to the beginning of the next.

Apart from batteries not primarily designed for eliciting linguistic information, batteries since QS have been far more homogeneous in respect of the linguistic features being tested. We are here primarily concerned with those hereafter referred to as Batteries I, II and III. For the most part they were designed to investigate certain aspects of adverbial use and Battery I dealt exclusively with such problems, paying close attention to the multiple use of an adverb (as disjunct, conjunct, or adjunct, to adopt the distinction in Greenbaum 1969a). For this purpose, certain common adverbs were used several times with varying degrees of differing function; in 16 sentences, two adverbs were used in a somewhat similar sentence frame and in eight of them the same adverb appeared twice in order to test the extent of contrast recognised by subjects. For example,

1. /hŏnestly# /Mr Jones honestly reported our stòry#
2. /rĕally# the /students réally wòrk during the term#

Furthermore, in attempting to achieve maximum comparability in results, contrasting adverb uses and positions were tested in identical or near-identical lexical environments. For example, 'His sons completely managed the family business' (the first sentence in the battery) and 'His sons managed the family business completely' (the 26th sentence).

The test was successful to a great extent in that subjects introduced fewer changes in sentences (1) and (2) above than in (3), where the two adverbs are in a more tautologous relation:

3. /neverthelĕss# /some people neverthelèss attempted it#

Thus, one of the instances of *nevertheless* was omitted by 11 out of 85 subjects, whereas with *honestly* and *really* omissions were made by only two and three subjects respectively. An attempt had been made to counteract any tendency to monotony by changing the frequency with which we switched from announcing the task first to announcing the sentence first; instead of keeping the procedure constant for blocks of ten, we narrowed the variation down to blocks of two. Useful in itself, this innovation could not of course offset the repetitiveness of linguistic pattern, which tended to invalidate the results. For example, in several instances where a sentence had two different adverbs (as in 'Frankly, the workers were honestly answered by the manager'), subjects responded with a sentence which had two instances of the same adverb ('Frankly . . . frankly . . .') instead. Moreover, so habituated did subjects become to having two adverbs in sentences that in three cases where they were given sentences having only one adverb, they added a second one. In one case, in fact, this addition resulted in two uses of the same adverb, so that 'His sons managed the family business completely' became 'His sons completely managed the family business completely', though this may result from the earlier occurrence of the sentence, in which *completely* was preverbal.

It was therefore decided to re-introduce greater variety into later batteries, especially so far as sentence pattern, lexical variety and type of sentence deviance are concerned. On our reading of the results of Battery III, it seems to us that a satisfactory balance has been struck between a degree of homogeneity that yields useful quantities of comparable linguistic data, and on the other hand a variation of sentence content and pattern that prevents subjects from having the feeling that there is repetition. The nearest we came to pattern similarity was with the following three sentences, which were widely scattered throughout the battery and which were accompanied by only one or two other sets showing similarity:

you could /always send it this afternŏon#
you should /always take it before dìnner#
they could /always go there tomòrrow#

The re-ordering experiments (see below, *p* 32) gave us no reason to suspect that memory of earlier instances in the above cases had a vitiating effect on the results.

Another problem concerns the interval provided for subjects' responses. In QS, constant intervals were measured from the beginning of one test announcement to the beginning of the next. This resulted in the subjects having in effect a variable interval for deciding on and registering their responses, depending on the length of the sentence and details of task. We altered the procedure so as to give a constant interval for the registration of responses.

In Battery I we tried to establish the optimum period of silence by providing intervals (25 seconds) which we could be sure were more than adequate, and by asking subjects to measure the free time they had between the completion of each task and the next announcement. As a result we were able to settle on an interval length of 15 seconds for subsequent batteries, irrespective of the length of the sentence, and the difficulty arising through sentence deviance and task complexity. In Battery II, for example, the range included

The girl frowned faintly.   →present

and

John broke the window, but he refused to pay for it.   → question

While the new interval appears adequate for the second of these tests, one cannot easily establish how much undesirable surplus time occurs with tests like the first. Many factors are involved in the time subjects 'require' for a particular task, and the advantages to the investigator (and probably subject alike) of a constant time interval outweigh any disadvantages it has. From the subject's viewpoint, the main advantage is that he quickly learns how much time he has available to perform each task and so settles into a regular work rhythm. From the investigator's viewpoint, a variable interval would involve intolerably arbitrary decisions.

With the judgment tests too, a comparable change was made in the timing procedure. With the evaluation tests, we settled on intervals of three seconds' duration between sentences. For the similarity tests, where two sentences had to be compared, five-second intervals were established. Some variation in the intervals was introduced for the preference tests. For most tests, in which two sentences had to be rated and ranked, 15-second intervals were allowed, but 20-second intervals were given for tests in which three sentences were involved. Furthermore, for the first couple of sentences subjects were allowed the longer interval of 20 seconds, since it was observed that they needed more time at the beginning of the series of preference tests to become familiar with the test procedure.

A major innovation in the presentation of tests since QS is that pre-liminary explanations and the tests themselves have been pre-recorded on tape and then relayed to the subjects. The advantage of a tape-recording over a 'live' reading is that it provides a better control over the timing of intervals and over the prosodic rendering of the sentences, in-cluding tempo, loudness, intonation, *etc.* In some of the tests in batteries since QS the choice of intonation is crucial. For example, it was essential for the particular purpose of the test that the sentence

/pĕrsonally# /I pĕrsonally# ap/prŏved of the idea#

should be read with an intonation break between the second *personally* and *approved* and that the second *personally* should carry a falling-rising nuclear tone. With a tape-recording, mistakes in the reading can be corrected before the experiment. If the investigator merely reads his tests to a group, he may make mistakes without noticing them; and if he does notice them, he may make matters worse by attempting a correction, thus affecting the validity of the results. Moreover, a recording ensures that different groups of subjects have the tests presented in precisely the same manner, and any imperfections in the recording, human or mech-anical, affect all subjects alike. A serious disadvantage, however, is that we have not always been able to use the same room for testing, and while an experienced speaker standing in front of an audience automatically adjusts to variable acoustic conditions, a recording cannot be adjusted with the same delicacy. It is therefore clear that experiments should be conducted under good acoustic conditions and, when practicable, in the same room.

A beneficial concomitant effect of the use of a tape-recording should be mentioned. The recording helps to create a more impersonal atmosphere, inducing a serious attitude to the experiment. Moreover, although as we shall see below (Chapter 6) the identity of a person present conducting the experiment has a considerable influence upon the results obtained, such effects would doubtless be even greater and less controllable if the subjects felt any temptation to attribute authorship of the test sentences to a person present, as they might well do if he were personally reading them.

Several steps towards analogous standardisation of procedures have been taken with judgment testing. A minor change since QS has been to issue duplicated sheets listing the test numbers with boxed spaces in which the responses are to be written. The preparation of this sheet led to the idea of stencilling on them in addition the criteria for judgment and the corresponding response symbols which hitherto were chalked on a blackboard, with natural variation from occasion to occasion and with more difficulty for the subjects who had to look up from time to time to refresh their memory; indeed, ability to see the board from where they sat might seriously vary also. With the preference tests, where the sentences were presented visually, it was natural to stencil not merely the test sentences but also the criteria for judgment and the corresponding symbols. We therefore put each judgment task on a separate page, together with the spaces indicated for responses; the pages were stapled together and on the cover of the booklet thus formed there was the instruction 'Please do not turn over this page until you are asked to'. The pages were then turned at timed intervals, as indicated above.

We now turn to changes in explanations and instructions that have been introduced since QS. Since the illustrative sentences were all non-deviant and since no warning was given to avoid introducing more changes than the task instruction actually specified, it could be objected that the results would not distinguish between subjects who had felt free (or even encouraged) to accompany the task operation by a linguistic smoothing in the direction of rectification and those who had felt constrained from doing so. We finally decided to introduce the following instruction to clarify the position: 'When you hear sentences out of context, they often sound strange. I want to emphasise that you should make only the changes that the instructions specify'.

We also decided that comparability of results would be improved if subjects were given practice in what was required of them before the batteries proper began. This question, along with discussion of the explicit instruction, is taken up in some detail below (Chapter 4).

We continued to preserve the anonymity of subjects, adding only to the request for regional background the request for information on sex and profession. Since our subjects are virtually always undergraduate students, the latter point in effect means their field of study and the stage they have reached. We also continued the practice of explaining the tasks by giving only a single non-deviant example with each task. From this point of view, a change from past to present was treated separately from one of present to past; a question involving inversion of elements already present (*he is coming – is he coming?*) separately from one involving the use of *do* (*he went – did he go?*). We did however move towards a greater degree of generality in referring to both the latter as '*yes* or *no* questions' rather than specifying (as in QS) the auxiliary with which the question should begin.

An experiment was carried out in one battery to find out if subjects not trained in linguistics could make adequate responses on considerably more abbreviated and generalised instructions. In this experiment, the abstraction 'change of tense' (with examples) was used, and questions were referred to without explaining the distinctive '*yes* or *no*' type. These and similar abbreviations appeared to result in no reduced understanding on the part of students of such disparate disciplines as medicine and English literature. In the same experiment, some extension of the range of tasks was tried out. As well as turning statements into questions, the converse was required; as well as making verbs present or past, the future was introduced (unanimously identified with *will/shall* by subjects, incidentally).

In Batteries I–III, the range of tasks remained as in QS, with some extension of the 'replacement type'. It came to include not merely subject pronouns of contrasting number but also of person, and in addition other elements than subject pronouns were involved in replacement. For example a complement pronoun had to be replaced by another pronoun; a noun phrase by a pronoun; one noun phrase premodifier by another; one verb by another; one adjunct by another; *etc.* The additional complexity of task was in part occasioned by greater complexity in the structure of test sentences. This has allowed us to ask (for example) for replacement of subordinate subjects and for negation of a specified verb in a sentence having more than one finite verb.

There has been only one important change in the instructions affecting the judgment tests. The middle term between 'normal' and 'abnormal' in the evaluation test was in QS specified as 'Marginal or dubious'. In Battery I, this was replaced by 'Not sure' (or 'Can't decide' in an experiment with oral responses: Davy and Quirk 1969) in case the term 'marginal' was too technical or too formal for non-linguist subjects. It was later however decided that subjects might feel that 'Not sure' reflected on their own inability to make their minds up rather than on the intermediate status of the sentence. We therefore settled on the middle term 'Somewhere between', which appears to be a more accurate specification of what we are seeking than any other single expression would be. The fact remains however that we are dissatisfied with judgment test response categories between the polar extremes. It is at least arguable that we need a four-point scale which could include with the 'Somewhere between' response (where the response implies an equal decisiveness on the subject's part) a response 'Not sure' which would allow the subject to indicate that decisiveness is precisely what he cannot feel. One experiment in Oregon along these lines, however, produced very much fewer 'Not sure' responses than 'Somewhere between', suggesting that at least little is lost by having only the latter as the middle term.

The technical aspects of the new tests introduced since QS will be described along with the description of the tests themselves later in this chapter. We should however mention that just as we have experimented with single-medium testing through aural-oral technique (as reported in Davy and Quirk 1969), so we have developed written single-medium forms of testing. We were primarily motivated by requiring a more complex set of judgment responses, and at the same time the written medium allowed us, when we wished, to confront subjects with a more complex set of linguistic data. Thus we were able to offer three sentences for comparison and request a preferential rating together with an evaluation of each sentence on the normal three-point scale. This visual technique will have an increasing independent value both for technical and for linguistic reasons. There is the problem, for example, of investigating longer stretches than the type of sentence that it is practicable to use in an oral battery and for conducting types of inquiry to which the oral battery is not adaptable. Again, we shall need to investigate the differing degrees of acceptability in written as distinct from spoken English.

The new types of performance test introduced since QS are not relevant to the present study, but a word must be added on the new types of judgment test, similarity and preference. The former were introduced first in Battery I, and as explained in Chapter 1 informants were asked to estimate the degree of similarity of meaning between two sentences. In most of the similarity tests, the two sentences were identical except for the position of an adverb, but in some tests a different adverb was used in each sentence; for example:

/rěally# your /children hòwl during the night#
your /children often hòwl during the night#

These tests have an obvious connexion with the 'two-adverb' sentences in the compliance and evaluation tests and were introduced to acquire data for comparison with these. A couple of tests were not concerned with adverbs but with differences in the placement of clause negation. Thus, subjects were required to judge the semantic affinity of the following pair of sentences:

I /don't think he's còming#
I /think he's not còming#

Preference tests were first used in a pilot experiment with one group taking Battery II. Sentences in two or three varying forms (each numbered) were written on a sliding blackboard in advance of the experiment. Each set of variants was made visible to subjects as required and then erased. Subjects were asked to look at the varying forms and then to indicate which form they preferred by writing down the number corresponding to the preferred form. They were allowed to write down more than one number if they felt no strong preference. In Battery III we introduced the use of stencilled booklets for preference tests. We then had a less cumbersome method of presenting sentences and at the same time we could incorporate many more tests than we could on a blackboard. Preference tests in Battery III were more complex. They required two sets of responses, *rating* and *ranking*, so that when a subject received the instruction to turn to the next page, he would be confronted by such a display as is illustrated in *Fig* 3.

Perfectly natural and normal = YES
Wholly unnatural and abnormal = NO
Somewhere between = ?

	Put YES, NO, or ?	Order of preference. Put 1, 2, 3
He doesn't have a car.	. . . .	. . . .
He hasn't a car.	. . . .	. . . .
He hasn't got a car.	. . . .	. . . .

Fig 3 : Specimen preference test

The mode of response is to some extent self-evident. In the first response column above, the rating for each sentence is in precisely the manner used in the ordinary evaluation test, the only difference being that one is now evoking visual acceptability rather than aural. In the second column, subjects ranked each sentence in relation to the others, with the provision that they might equate two or more; thus responses might be 1, 3, 2; 1, 1, 2; 2, 2, 1; *etc.* As with the similarity tests, we have here the facility to acquire data valuably correlatable with the results of the selection test on the one hand (*eg* in Battery III, preference test O1 with selection test O1) and with the results of the evaluation test on the other (though there are no examples where this happens to have been attempted). Not merely may visual evaluation differ from aural evaluation of the same sentence:

there may well be interesting differences between evaluation based on a single sentence and evaluation where two or more possibilities are simultaneously presented. Thus there is an inevitable interaction between the rating and ranking components.

But in addition to the three new types of test, some important new features were introduced into existing types of test. In QS, sentences were not affected in their non-deviance or their degree of deviance by the prescribed operation, and to that extent the operation tasks bore no specific relation to the test sentences and theoretically they could be interchanged. In Battery I, we introduced non-deviant sentences, the 'target' form of which would be seriously deviant as a result of a specific operation mechanically applied. For example:

He can certainly drive a car.   → negative

Clearly in this instance the problem depends on the negation task and indeed arises only from it; some alternative tasks such as tense change would not give rise to this problem. With the task as specified, the target sentence would be

He can not certainly drive a car.

and the interest of the test lies in the way subjects react to this emergence of deviance on operation, namely the position of adverbs like *certainly* ('disjuncts': Greenbaum 1969a) after the negative particle. In Battery III, we experimented with the converse of this: sentences which were deviant in their presentation form becoming non-deviant in their target form. For example:

She has mentioned it at all.   → question

It is of some interest to note that this latter type of problem appears to give subjects little trouble: in this specific instance, for only two out of 117 subjects were there results that were relevantly non-compliant ('RNC': see *p* 20). With the type of problem that, by contrast, appears only on operation there is a very different reaction: the requirement to negate *He can certainly drive a car* produced non-compliance scores from every single subject, and (as we shall see below) there is good evidence that the non-compliance rate from a situation in which the deviance emerges from the operation task will always be higher than when the deviance is already present in the test sentence. For example, the following test, with deviance on presentation,

Reluctantly, they don't insist on his resignation.   → past produced relevant non-compliances from 9/70 subjects whereas the following test, with identical deviance only on operation,

Reluctantly, they insisted on his resignation.   → negative

produced relevant non-compliances from 21/55 subjects ($p < \cdot005$).

Finally, where in QS sentences were presented for evaluation in their original test form, we have come to introduce the practice of presenting sentences in their target form. Clearly this had to be the situation for those sentences in which deviance appeared only on operation: otherwise we should have been inviting evaluation of irrelevantly non-deviant sentences. But we extended the principle to include sentences which were deviant already in their pre-operation form. The value of this procedure can be readily demonstrated. With D4 (Battery III) 'She deeply admired the speech', relevant non-compliances were recorded from 34/117 subjects. Now, if we had put the sentence in this form for evaluation we have no reason to believe that we would have had much less than 100 per cent acceptance. In this event, the fairly high incidence of relevant non-compliances would have been puzzling. But the operation task was 'Make this a question' and the evaluation form of the sentence was 'Did she deeply admire the speech?': this in fact received only 52/117 acceptance scores and thus drew our attention to the sharp difference in acceptability between *deeply admire* in declarative sentences and the same juxtaposition of the items in interrogative sentences. The point was therefore further investigated in a later experiment with a different task, and a comparison of the results is discussed in Chapter 8 (*p* 79).

The present study reports experimental work since QS to only a limited extent and for more specialised information reference should be made to the following sources: Greenbaum 1969a, 1969b and 1970; Davy and Quirk 1969; Quirk 1970a and 1970b; Kempson and Quirk 1970; Tottie (forthcoming).

Chapter 3

The relevant aspects
of responses

With the judgment tests the scoring is directly related to the subjects' responses in an obvious way and our present practice does not differ in principle from that established in QS. With the performance tests, on the other hand, radical developments have taken place in the scoring procedure and our practice needs to be stated in full. We shall first explain the scoring of compliance tests, as summarised in *Fig* 4.

Compliance	A	
Hesitation	B	peripheral
	C	central but not concerned with evasion
	D	concerned with evasion
Non-compliance	E	peripheral
	F	central but not evasive
	G	central and evasive
	O	total omission

RNC (bracketing G and O)

Fig 4: Scoring system

Compliance is defined as obedience to the instruction to perform a specific task on a specific test sentence, even where this would oblige a subject to produce a deviant sentence. Such obedience, without the introduction of additional changes, produces what we refer to as the 'target' sentence. Thus if the 'response' sentence (the sentence produced by the subject) is identical with the target sentence, it is scored as 'compliant'. We may decide in advance that the target sentence may have more than one form. For example, if the test is:

/lŭckily# the /game luckily ends at sèven#   → past

we may reckon as variant forms of target sentence:

Luckily, the game luckily ended at seven.
Luckily, the game has luckily ended at seven.
Luckily, the game had luckily ended at seven.

Non-compliance is defined as a failure to respond with the target sentence, including of course the failure to offer any response sentence at all. In addition to such total omission, three non-compliance types are recognised. These are based on the degree to which the response is relevant to the linguistic problem set up by the investigator.

G non-compliances represent evasions of the problem. For example, the test

he will /probably stay làte#   → question

would have the target sentence

Will he probably stay late?

The responses

Will he stay late?
Will he possibly stay late?
Is it probable that he will stay late?
He will probably stay late, won't he?

will be scored as G non-compliances since the linguistic problem is the presence of *probably* in a question, and all these responses represent an evasion of the problem.

G non-compliances and total omissions are taken to be the most *relevant* measure of *non-compliance* ('RNC'). It is the aggregate RNC scores that are normally used in this study as the non-compliance result.

F non-compliances are changes in the 'problem area' of the target sentence which do not however amount to an evasion of the problem. For example, the response sentence

Will he stay late probably?

would be so scored because although the subject has moved *probably* (that is, he has made a change in the problem area), he has still left *probably* in a question.

E non-compliances are changes which are totally peripheral to the problem (though at the same time they no doubt reflect the subject's unease). For example,

Will you probably stay late?
Will he probably stay?

If there is a hesitation (represented for example by overwriting or deletion) in connexion with any of these non-compliance types, such responses are distinguished as G?, F?, E? respectively.

In addition to noting the type and number of non-compliances in response sentences, we note in each case the mode of their realisation. Thus within each type of non-compliance, we distinguish the following realisation modes:

1. Partial omission: the subject makes a response but omits one or more words that would be present in the correct target sentence. A single response sentence may of course have omissions of more than one non-compliance type. To take an extreme example

   Will stay – ?

   has one E omission (*late*), one omission (*he*) which would be classed as F since it would seem to be connected with the interrogation problem, and one G omission (*probably*).

2. Addition: for example *now* in

   Will he now probably stay late?

3. Replacement: for example, *you* in

   Will you probably stay late?

4. Transposition: for example, of the adverb in

   Will he stay late probably?

5. Simple paradigmatic grammatical changes such as changes in tense or number in verbs, changes in number in nouns, a change from a declarative form of the sentence to an interrogative form, or from an affirmative to a negative form. For example, the negative transformation in

   Won't he probably stay late?

6. Structural reformulation such as is involved with voice transformation or other focus-shifting processes. For example,

   Is it probable that he will stay late?

It should be noted that changes under (5) and (6) will often necessarily involve changes that might otherwise have been registered under (1)–(4).

2

It should further be noted that a response which is identical with the test sentence (that is without the task being carried out) is scored as a non-compliance like any other response according to the way it differs from the target sentence. Thus

He will probably stay late.

as a non-compliance of the task to turn this into a question would be scored as a G non-compliance, realised in mode (5) above.

All hesitations are graded in a three-term typology similar to that for non-compliances. D denotes hesitations over whether the problem is to be evaded or not. For example

Will he ((probably)) stay late?

where our double parentheses represent deletion of the word. C is used for hesitations within the problem area which do not however suggest that the subject is hesitating over evading the problem. For example, confused hesitation over the spelling of *probably*. Finally, B type hesitations are quite outside the problem area. For example

Will he probably ⟨stay⟩ late?

where our diamond brackets represent later insertion. Hesitations are classed as D, C, or B irrespective of whether they result in compliance or non-compliance; thus at one extreme we may have a compliant response (normally scored as A) which is scored as A? on the grounds of having one or more hesitations, the ? being matched with a B, C or D score; at the other extreme we may have a total omission which has become total only as a result of deletion (scored of course as hesitation).

There are two additional ways in which hesitations are categorised (though within each type no further numerical account is taken): specifications and realisations. Hesitation *specifications* are five in number:

1. Errors in spelling or punctuation (which are regarded as 'hesitations' for scoring purposes).
2. Alterations in spelling or punctuation, whether they result in right or wrong forms.

These two are regarded as most trivial and cannot apply to type D. Hesitations that we regard as less trivial are categorised according to their 'direction': that is, according to whether they result in a greater or lesser approximation to the target sentence.

3. Hesitations in the direction of compliance. For instance, the insertion of *stay* in the example cited above.

4. Hesitations in the direction of non-compliance, as in the case of the deleted *probably* in the example cited earlier.
5. Hesitations in neither direction or where the direction is uncertain. The latter may be illustrated by illegibility, the former by such an example as

Will he probably ⟨remain⟩ late?

where the diamond brackets represent a hesitant insertion of a verb which replaces the one in the target sentence.

Hesitation *realisations* are again five in number:
1. overwriting
2. deletion
3. insertion
4. replacement (thus involving and subsuming 2 and 3)
5. overt indication of hesitation

This last may take the form of unfilled gaps in response sentences, parenthesised exclamation marks, underlining, or actual verbal comment. The provision of alternative versions is also regarded as overt hesitation.

In addition to the analysis of each form of non-compliance and hesitation, we make two kinds of impressionistic assessment for each non-compliant response sentence:
1. We assess the acceptability of the response sentence relative to that of the target sentence on a three-point scale:
   [*a*] the response sentence is more acceptable than the target sentence;
   [*b*] it is equally acceptable;
   [*c*] it is less acceptable.
2. We assess the degree of semantic equivalence between the response sentence and the target sentence, again on a three-point scale:
   [*a*] the response sentence is approximately the same in meaning as the target sentence;
   [*b*] it is somewhat different in meaning;
   [*c*] it is sharply different in meaning.

The other types of performance test require different scoring procedures. The distinction between 'compliant' and 'non-compliant' is not relevant to selection or completion tests, though with selection tests, we can make use of *categorisation* of non-compliance or hesitation already described. In selection tests, we are chiefly concerned however to record which of two or more forms the subject uses at the relevant point in the target sentence. For example in the test

None of the children answered the question.   → present

we are interested in learning whether the subject will use the singular
form of the verb or the plural. Only 'valid' responses concern us. Thus
the chief information we need to score is which of the forms occurs in each
response sentence, as distinct from an irrelevant response such as (in this
instance)

None of the children can answer the question.

It may be noted at this point that the principle of recording 'selection
variables' is applicable in certain cases to compliance tests where we
wish to use responses to accumulate information that is only incidental
to the specific test.

In addition to scoring data of direct linguistic interest on the foregoing
lines, we preserve information on subjects and test procedures. Although,
as already stated, we deliberately avoid implicating a subject by his
identity, we ask each one to state some general biographical data: sex,
area of upbringing, precise professional activity (*eg* second-year
chemistry student at University College London), acceptability-testing
experience (though in fact we have not so far used any subjects for more
than one test). The most important test-procedure data to be mentioned here are: the test category; the task; whether the task or the test
sentence was announced first; the order in which the tests were presented
(where a battery exists in more than one order); the identification number
of the subject and of the group in which he took the test. Each of these
items of information is preserved with each response sentence and the
scoring details as outlined above. All the data of Battery III have been
punched on IBM cards and the numerical (including statistical) information in this monograph is derived from programs devised by our
colleague Caroline Bott for analysing these data on the University College
London IBM 360/65. Moreover, work is in progress on correlation programs which will examine the co-occurrence of items from different information classes. For example, we can if we wish investigate the modes
of hesitation realisation occurring along with G non-compliances in a
particular test. Or we may wish to know how the individual's judgment
responses correlate with his performance responses in respect of a particular linguistic feature. Again, we may seek to establish the patterns of
non-compliance to be found in whole categories of test sentence. Such
inquiries are naturally extremely laborious to achieve by other than
computational means. The first achievement of the correlation program
has been to compare the performance of male and female subjects in
respect of G non-compliance scores. As one might expect, the G scores

for the majority of the tests are distributed proportionately between the sexes, but with a small number of tests a significant difference between the men and women was observed.[1] Females had significantly higher G scores in three tests:

A15 (III) $p < \cdot 025$
F10 (III) $p = \cdot 05$
X3 (IIIa) $p < \cdot 025$

Males had significantly higher G scores in four tests:

U1 (III) $p = \cdot 05$
Z1 (III) $p < \cdot 005$
N3 (IIIa) $p < \cdot 01$
U1 (IIIa) $p < \cdot 001$

It is noteworthy that a significant difference is found twice with U1, one of the few tests which is exactly repeated in Batteries III and IIIa. We shall not, however, speculate here on the reasons for the sex-conditioned differences in results; in the case of X3 the problem is further investigated in Quirk 1970a.

---

[1] Throughout this study, the χ^2 test has been applied to results being compared. A level of at least five per cent ($p \leqslant \cdot 05$) has been considered significant. Yates's correction for continuity has been applied in all cases where the number of degrees of freedom is one.

Chapter 4

Testing the test design

We have examined four principle variables of test design that might be expected to affect the reliability of the experimental results. Doubtless the least important of these is the relative order of test sentence and task instructions in performance tests.

TASK–SENTENCE ORDER

We have already mentioned in Chapter 2 our change from QS in this respect. Our procedure has in general been to alternate in sets of two as between announcing the sentence first and announcing the task first. The relative order of task and sentence is indicated in the task column of the tabular appendices by the prefix 'T' for task first and 'S' for sentence first. There is little to show that either order presented subjects with more difficulty than the other, but there is one apparent exception. Tests D_1 and D_4 (III) have almost identical ratings in the evaluation test, and this is what one would intuitively expect:

Did he badly need the money?
Did she deeply admire the speech?

In the compliance test both sentences were tested with the same operation and with the same permutations in sequence. In fact the only considerable variable was the task–sentence order; in D_1 the task was given first and in D_4 the sentence was given first. All five groups show a higher RNC rate corresponding to the order task–sentence: $65/117$ for D_1 as compared with $34/117$ for D_4 (a discrepancy of 27 per cent). These results may, however, reflect a difference in acceptability not detected in the evaluation test. Certainly, the other tests where comparison is possible yield no differences of this order. In Batteries II and III, the same test

(H11 *He will probably stay late* $\rightarrow$ question) occurred, having sentence first in II and task first in III; the RNCs were 49/179 (27 per cent) in II and 27/117 in III (a discrepancy of only four per cent).

If even such small differences as these are attributable to variation in task–sentence presentation, one would require good evidence of the independent value of such variation in technique to justify its retention. No such value has been demonstrated. It was introduced to prevent habituation in the subjects' responses and we feel that this essential feature is adequately achieved by varying degrees and categories of sentence deviance and by adding to the variety of tasks (as we have done, for example, by introducing the completion test).

In future, then, we would suggest having a single task–sentence procedure, and the question arises as to which is preferable. We should naturally want a procedure which maximally obliges (or enables) subjects to grasp the structure of the test sentence as a whole, and one might suppose that this is best achieved if the sentence is given first and only afterwards the instruction as to what the subjects are to do with it. Most of the results we have scrutinised give little or no indication in confirmation or denial of this, but there is one piece of evidence which powerfully suggests denial. In Battery II, M2 and M3 differed in having task–sentence and sentence–task order respectively. Both sentences began with a 'pendant participle' and in both cases the task was to make the verb past tense. With one of the sentences (M2), two per cent of subjects (four) misperformed the task by making not only the finite verb past but by altering the present participle to its perfective form ('Having walked . . .'). With the other, a much higher proportion, 15 per cent (27 subjects), made non-compliant responses of this kind; instead of 'Living in London . . .', one subject in fact began his response with the nonsensical 'Was living . . .'. It is to be supposed that misperformances here indicate that subjects have perceived the structure of the sentence on which they are working only to a relatively low or superficial degree: that, in other words, they are mechanically applying the tense-change task before or in the absence of a full grasp of the sentence. The extent to which such a superficial approach follows from a specific task–sentence presentation order would surely be a measure of the undesirability of this order. While one might have supposed the converse aprioristically, the order with the greatest number of such misperformances is that in which the sentence is presented first, followed by the task-instruction. In another example (M4, II), beginning 'Seriously speaking', this order apparently led one subject to begin his tense-change operation with the morphologically deviant 'Seriously speaked'. We therefore have no hesitation in deciding that in future only one order should be used in acceptability testing, and that to specify the *task* first and to follow this with the sentence on which it is to be performed will lead to linguistically more significant results.

EXPLICIT INSTRUCTION

In QS as well as in Batteries I and II, it was hoped that the instructions implied that subjects should carry out the tasks prescribed without introducing other changes which might, for example, 'rectify' a sentence. With the sixth group of subjects that took Battery II (a group of teachers) it was decided to experiment with making this explicit for the following reasons:

1. Since the instructions already implied that subjects should do no more than they were told to do, we considered that by giving an explicit instruction to this effect we would not be introducing a new factor.
2. Some individuals had asked us for specific assurance on this point.
3. It was possible to devise a form of explicit instruction that would not draw informants' attention to the fact that they were going to face deviant sentences.

We therefore predicted that we would lose little by way of 'over-rectification' and would gain in knowing that the only rectification occurring would be that which subjects felt unable to resist and would not include rectification which a few subjects might mistakenly feel was expected of them.

Group 6, n(umber) = 34, was divided so that while 16 received only the old 'implicit' instruction, 18 had an additional 'explicit' instruction as follows: 'Sentences heard in isolation often sound strange. We would emphasise that you should make only the changes that the instructions specify.' No subject knew that two different forms of instruction were in use.

The difference in the form of instruction appears to have an important effect on the responses. With the 18 sentences which are deviant on presentation, the subjects who have the explicit instruction $(+E)$ make significantly fewer RNCs:

$$-E \: \frac{115}{288} \qquad\qquad +E \: \frac{64}{324}$$

$$p < \cdot 001$$

This of course is easy to explain and indeed what one might expect: subjects noticed the deviant sentences but in view of the explicit instruction tended to resist any temptation to alter them. With the 14 sentences which were non-deviant on presentation but which would become deviant on strict application of the operation task, a significant difference in results emerged which is less easy however to account for:

$$-\text{E } \frac{111}{224} \qquad\qquad +\text{E } \frac{150}{252}$$

$$p < \cdot 05$$

It will be observed that with these sentences, subjects who had the explicit instruction actually made more RNCs than those without this instruction. We would suggest that this is because the explicit instruction might have suggested that consequential changes were not merely to be tolerated but perhaps expected of them. Thus with a sentence that might be regarded as deviant on presentation, such as in L2 (II):

She's very clever, between you and I.   → negative

it appears that the explicit instruction assures subjects that they need not, indeed instructs them that they should not, alter *I* to *me* in the course of performing the task. But with a sentence such as in F5 (II):

She has wisely refused your offer.   → negative

where the mechanical performance would yield 'She has not wisely refused your offer', it may be supposed that the explicit instruction has made subjects feel they may (perhaps ought to) offer as the transformed sentence

She has wisely not refused your offer.

or

Wisely she has not refused your offer.

regarding these consequential transpositions (not unreasonably) as falling within the formula of 'changes that the instructions specify'. The same trend can perhaps be observed in the only other evidence we can produce for the effect of the explicit instruction. This is as follows. In view of the results of the experiment with Battery II Group 6, we decided to introduce the explicit instruction as a general procedure in the future. This means that all Battery III results are obtained under these conditions. But one test sentence (H11) in Battery II was repeated with the same operation in Battery III; the RNCs for subjects whose conditions were strictly comparable were as follows (showing no significant difference):

$$-\text{E } \frac{35}{145}\,(24\%) \qquad\qquad +\text{E } \frac{27}{99}\,(27\%)$$

PRACTICE

Practice in handling operations has three distinct aspects: (i) experience in performing the tasks, (ii) awareness that deviant sentences are being presented, and (iii) becoming used to the time intervals allowed for performing the tasks. It is important to distinguish these factors which concern the results of tests near the beginning of a battery from two purely sequence factors: the effect of an immediately preceding test and habituation to a particular problem category. Both these are discussed below in the section on Order Variation. Battery III was tested with two groups of subjects, A and B (each $n = 18$), differing only according as one group began by having a practice run of ten sentences devised ad hoc for the purpose. The subjects who had this degree of practice ($+P$) made significantly fewer RNCs than those who had not had practice. The results for the whole battery contrast as follows:

$$-P \frac{199}{450} \qquad\qquad +P \frac{150}{450}$$
$$p < \cdot 005$$

Within the battery, one small group of tests seems to reflect the contrast particularly sharply. The tests in question (nine in all) are those which were non-deviant on presentation but which became deviant on strict application of the task instructions:

$$-P \frac{79}{162} \qquad\qquad +P \frac{58}{162}$$
$$p < \cdot 025$$

Thus it would seem clear that practice helps subjects to avoid the temptation of introducing the additional changes necessary to correct or avoid deviance. The above distinction is confirmed in the results of Battery II Group 6, which in addition to being divided as between explicit or non-explicit (as explained above), had a cross-division as between 'practice' and 'non-practice', thus producing a four-way division $+P+E$, $+P-E$, $-P+E$, $-P-E$. The two $+E$ subgroups (each $n = 9$) are thus strictly comparable with Groups A and B in Battery III. The results for the Battery II subgroups in respect of 14 sentences non-deviant on presentation but becoming deviant on operation are as follows:

$$-P \frac{83}{126} \qquad\qquad +P \frac{67}{126}$$
$$p = \cdot 05$$

PRACTICE AND EXPLICITNESS

We have considered both practice and the explicit instruction separately as independent variables. All the data supplied on practice are derived

from groups which have had the explicit instruction, and all the data
supplied on the effect of explicitness are derived from groups where we
could hold the practice/non-practice factor constant and compare only
like with like. We have now to consider the extent to which these two
variables interact.

We have seen that with sentences becoming deviant only on operation
the chances of RNC scores are increased both if there has been no
practice and also if subjects have received the explicit instruction. We
should expect that if both these conditions were present they would rein-
force each other and produce a still stronger tendency towards RNC.
This is clearly borne out by the quartered experiment with Group 6
(Battery II):

$-P$	$-P$	$+P$	$+P$
$+E$	$-E$	$+E$	$-E$
$\frac{83}{126}$	$\frac{68}{126}$	$\frac{67}{126}$	$\frac{43}{98}$

Comparing the extremes, the first and last columns, we have a significant
difference ($p < \cdot005$). It will be noted that the two middle columns show
close similarity and that they fall midway between the extremes. This is
readily attributable to the neutralising effect in each case of there being
present both a factor encouraging increased RNC and a factor encouraging reduced RNC.

With sentences that are deviant on presentation we have seen that the
explicit instruction again reduces RNC. The interaction with practice
however produces complication:

$+P$	$-P$	$-P$	$+P$
$-E$	$-E$	$+E$	$+E$
$\frac{64}{126}$	$\frac{51}{162}$	$\frac{39}{162}$	$\frac{25}{162}$

From what has been said, it is no surprise that the extremes here (the first
and last columns, with a significant difference: $p < \cdot001$) correspond to
' $-E$ ' and ' $+E$ ' respectively. What needs explanation is that both extremes have ' $+P$ '. It would seem that in the absence of the explicit
instruction, practice will merely result in improving the subjects' ability
to rectify a deviant sentence (that is, increasing the number of RNCs).[1]
On the other hand, where subjects have been expressly told not to rectify,

---

[1] Where subjects encounter deviant sentences repeatedly of the same category,
this should be regarded rather as 'experience' than as 'practice' from the present
viewpoint. As we shall see in considering the re-ordering experiments, such
experience results in habituation and hence reduction of RNCs.

practice will enable them to comply the more efficiently, thus reducing the RNCs.

The absence of practice will reduce the extreme effect of the presence or absence of the explicit instruction. Thus the group that was given an explicit instruction will in this case have more RNCs than the comparable group with practice, while the group that was not given an explicit instruction will have less RNCs than the group with practice. In both cases the presence of practice increases the effectiveness of the $+E$ or $-E$ factor.

Since as we shall see below (p 90) a test may yield a particular result merely on account of its occurring very early in the battery, it is clear that the first few tests on any occasion provide in effect practice. We thus have the possibility of offsetting the skew effect of early position in the battery by including a set of practice sentences whose results can be ignored. It is for this reason that we recommend providing subjects with practice before compliance tests. Indeed, although we have not sought evidence on the point, the judgment tests could no doubt also be improved by the provision of practice.

ORDER VARIATION

The tests in Batteries I, IIIa, and IV were given in only one order, but with Batteries II and III we investigated the effect upon results of presenting the test sentences in two orders. The tests of Battery IV are listed in Tables 15 and 16 in their presentation order, but for the other batteries the tables list the tests in the order of linguistic category, as defined and explained in Chapter 7. The presentation order for the tests of these batteries can be ascertained as follows. For Battery I, Tables 1 and 8 indicate the sequence number in a column alongside the category number. For Batteries II and III, the sequence adopted for Order (i) and Order (ii) in each case is given in Tables 17 and 18 respectively. The tests in Battery IIIa followed the sequence of Battery III Order (i).

In devising Order (ii) for Battery II we took the last 25 sentences en bloc and placed them before what had been the first 25 sentences in Order (i), so that the Order (i) sequence of 1–50 became in Order (ii) a sequence corresponding to the original numbers 26–50, 1–25. With Battery III, however, we devised the Order (ii) by independently reversing each of the original sequences 1–25 and 26–50, so that the Order (i) sequence of 1–50 became in Order (ii) a sequence corresponding to the original numbers 25–1, 50–26. With both batteries, some groups of subjects were given the tests in Order (i) and other groups in Order (ii), as indicated in the tabular appendices. It should be noted, however, that in the comparisons that follow we have excluded from consideration (so far as results are concerned) the groups who were involved in the practice and explicit instruction experiments and whose results are therefore not strictly comparable with those of the other groups on the basis of order variation alone. For judgment results, order variation provides the sole relevant variable for all groups.

Battery II

Performance tests—Compliance:
   The results from the two orders were in agreement over 39 of the 42 tests, the exceptions being
   A10 $p < .05$
   A12 $p < .001$
   M3 $p < .05$

Performance tests—Selection:
   The two orders were in agreement over the four tests in respect *both* of majority and minority selection forms.

Judgment tests—Evaluation:
   For the plus scores, there was agreement over 46 of the 51 tests, the exceptions being
   K1 $p < .05$
   L1 $p < .025$
   L2 $p < .05$
   N2 $p < .005$
   R1 $p < .005$
   For the minus scores, there was agreement over 45 tests, the exceptions being
   F8 $p < .025$
   K1 $p < .05$
   L1 $p < .025$
   L2 $p < .025$
   N2 $p < .001$
   R1 $p < .01$
   The presence of a small number in F8 is of course a distorting factor, making the significance test unreliable.

Judgment test—Similarity:
   There were ten tests. For the equals scores, the two orders agreed over nine, the exception being
   A11 $p < .025$

For the non-equals scores, there was again agreement over nine tests, the exception being

A13 $p < \cdot 05$

Battery III

Performance tests—Compliance:

The results for the two orders were in agreement over 25 of the 30 tests, the exceptions being

A15 $p < \cdot 001$
B13 $p < \cdot 025$
D1 $p < \cdot 05$
G4 $p < \cdot 005$
L3 $p < \cdot 05$

For B13, G4 and L3, the presence of small numbers is a distorting factor.

Performance tests—Selection:

There were 16 tests and the orders agreed over 15 of them for both majority and minority selected forms, the exception being

N7 $p < \cdot 005$ for both majority and minority selection.

Judgment tests—Evaluation:

For the plus scores, there was agreement over 27 of the 32 tests, the exceptions being

D1 $p < \cdot 05$
G4 $p < \cdot 001$
S1 $p < \cdot 01$
U2 $p < \cdot 05$
Z1 $p < \cdot 025$

For the minus scores, there was agreement over 23 of the 32 tests, the exceptions being

D1 $p < \cdot 001$
D2 $p < \cdot 01$
D5 $p < \cdot 001$
F10 $p < \cdot 05$
G4 $p < \cdot 025$
L3 $p < \cdot 05$
N6 $p < \cdot 05$
U1 $p < \cdot 05$
U2 $p < \cdot 025$

For D1 and U1, the presence of small numbers is a distorting factor.

Judgment tests—Similarity:
There were seven tests and agreement was shown over six of them, in
respect of both equals and non-equals responses, the exception being
A17 $p < .005$ (for equals)
$p < .05$ (for non-equals)
Judgment tests—Preference:
There was agreement over all the variant forms presented in 14 of the
15 tests in respect of the 'first preference' scores. The one exception
concerns the 'first preference' ranking of *does not need to go* (W1b),
$p < .025$.

SUMMARY

While there is, of course, predominant agreement between the two orders
both for Battery II and Battery III, there are more exceptions than we
shall find in comparing group results within each order (Chapter 5), and
it would seem that order is clearly an important variable in test conditions. Thus with Battery II compliance results, the significantly different
results for the three tests as between the two orders is undoubtedly
attributable to the effect of sequence; this can be seen by looking at the
scatter of results within each order for these sentences (A10, A12, M3) in
Table 17. We would therefore conclude that we need to present each
battery in more than one order. So far we have experimented with two
types of re-ordering. The type of re-ordering in Battery II provides a
contrast between early, central, and late experience of test sentences, but
it has the disadvantage of leaving almost every sentence unchanged in
respect of which sentence immediately precedes it. It is possible, for example, that the surprising difference between test sentences of the same
deviance type is to be explained with reference to the preceding sentence:
eg B13. This was predicted to be a non-deviant control sentence and in
Order (i) this was confirmed by there being no RNCs; in Order (ii), however, there were six RNCs. The difference cannot be explained by a
different general position in the battery according to the two orders (it
was number 37 and 39 respectively), but when we look at the immediately
preceding sentence that occurred with the two orders, an explanation suggests itself. Whereas in Order (i), it is preceded by a non-deviant sentence
(G2), in Order (ii) it was preceded by D5, not merely very deviant but
deviant in respect of adverb preceding verb, just as *totally* preceded
rejected in B13. The re-ordering in Battery III is superior in remedying
the disadvantage present in the Battery II re-ordering since no sentence
is immediately preceded by the identical sentence in the two orders.

However it has the disadvantage that sentences bearing the numbers around 13 and 38 in the first ordering will be again placed approximately a quarter and three-quarters way through the battery respectively on the re-ordering. It is fair to add that we know of no ill effects that this factor has had on the results, and this influences our recommendation for future batteries. Neither of the above re-orderings has ensured that tests dealing with the same type of deviance are given two re-orderings, such that the one ordering is the reversal of the other. This could be achieved readily by a 50–1 re-ordering and the sole disadvantage (that the 'middle' sentences would still be 'middle' sentences) is probably of no importance.

Chapter 5

Comparability and consistency

All our subjects are native speakers of English, educated to university standard; indeed all our groups have consisted of students undergoing university courses. This has meant that in general our groups consist of undergraduates around the age of 20, the only notable exception being a group of graduate teachers of English taking a short in-service course in London. The restriction to university-educated subjects is deliberate; the virtual restriction to young people reflects the easy availability of such subjects and the difficulty of conducting experiments with comparable groups of older people. Within this restriction, however, we have sought to obtain responses from as varied a body of students as is conveniently possible, a matter which is doubly easy at the University of Londo where not merely a wide range of disciplines is available but where a wide range of regional, school and social backgrounds is represented. The subjects have largely been British, but there have been several from the United States and the Commonwealth. Those involved in the batteries to be discussed, all members of University College London unless otherwise specified, took the tests in groups as follows:

Battery I

Group 1 (n=29): First-year students specialising in Geography.

Group 2 (n=29): First-year students specialising in English Literature.

Group 3 (n=27): First-year students specialising in Engineering.

Battery II

Group 1 (n=31): Second-year students specialising in several different Arts subjects.

Group 2 (n=50): First-year medical students.

Group 3 (n = 26):   Mixed undergraduate group, specialising in
                    several different Arts subjects.
Group 4 (n = 17):   Mixed undergraduate group of Arts and
                    Science students.
Group 5 (n = 21):   Second-year women students specialising in
                    English Literature at Bedford College,
                    London.
Group 6 (n = 34):   Graduate teachers of English engaged on a
                    short linguistics course at the Institute of
                    Education, London, with an average of
                    15 years' teaching experience.

Battery III
Group D (n = 33):   First-year students, chiefly women and chiefly
                    specialising in English Literature at Bedford
                    College, London.
Group E (n = 22):   First-year students specialising in German.
Group C (n = 26):   First-year students (mainly women) specialising
                    in English Literature at Westfield College,
                    London.
Group B (n = 18)⎫   First-year students specialising in English
Group A (n = 18)⎬   Literature.

Battery IIIa
Group F (n = 70):   Chiefly first-year students each specialising in
                    three Arts subjects, one being Linguistics, at
                    Reading University.

Battery IV
Group Eng (n = 20)⎫ First-year students specialising in English
Group Sci (n = 20)⎬ Literature.

GROUP COMPARABILITY
We have already explained the restriction upon the population from
which the foregoing groups have been drawn. The question now arises as
to the extent to which any of these groups is an adequate sample of the
population of university students. Practical considerations made the
demands of a strict statistical sampling procedure out of the question, but
we may reasonably inquire about the comparability of one group with
another and – beyond this – the degree to which the different groups
complement each other.

   In what follows, we shall ignore the three groups who took Battery I
since the experience of this battery led us to improve the structure and

presentation procedures with later batteries. We shall concentrate therefore on the groups who took Batteries II and III, restricting detailed consideration to the major test components, compliance and evaluation.

The groups that are directly comparable are:

[a] Groups 1, 2 and 3 who took Battery II in the Order (i) version, the
tests following the sequence shown in the second column of Table
17.

[b] Groups 4, 5 and 6 who took Battery II in the Order (ii) version
(sequence shown in third column of Table 17); Group 6 have
additional variables not merely as teachers but in respect of 'practice' and 'explicit instruction', discussed above, pp 28–32; for the
latter reason their compliance test results are here ignored.

[c] Groups D and E, who took Battery III in the Order (i) version
(sequence shown in the second column of Table 18).

[d] Groups C, B and A who took Battery III in the Order (ii) version
(sequence shown in the third column of Table 18). The 'practice'
variable rules out the inclusion of Group A's compliance results
(see p 30).

The [a] Groups

Compliance tests: there are 42 tests altogether and the RNC scores for
33 of these show no differences reaching a significance level of ·05.
The nine tests where groups vary significantly in their RNC
scores are as follows:

A10 $p < ·05$
A11 $p < ·05$
A12 $p < ·025$
A14 $p < ·025$
H6 $p < ·025$
H13 $p < ·025$
M1 $p < ·001$
Q1 $p < ·05$
R3 $p < ·05$

It is worth mentioning that with all except H6 the significance level
is artificially increased by the occurrence of very small numbers
(three or less) in one of the cells of the χ^2 table.

Evaluation tests: out of 51 tests, the groups agree for plus scores in 49
cases; the exceptions are

K1 $p < ·005$
M1 $p < ·05$

both having the distorting effect of small numbers. For the minus
scores, again 49 tests show agreement, the exceptions being:

L1 $p < \cdot025$
M2 $p < \cdot05$

The [b] Groups

Compliance tests: over the 42 tests, the groups are in agreement in
their RNC scores for 41 of them. The exception is

R3 $p < \cdot05$

with the distorting effect of small numbers.

Evaluation tests: with the plus scores, the groups agree in 46 of the 51
tests, the exceptions being

A9 $p < \cdot05$
F8 $p < \cdot025$
H10 $p < \cdot05$
J4 $p < \cdot05$
M2 $p < \cdot005$

H10 being the only one not subject to the distorting effect of small
numbers. With the minus scores, the groups agree over 49 tests, the
exceptions being:

L2 $p < \cdot05$
M2 $p < \cdot005$

The second of these is subject to the distorting effect of small
numbers. In both cases it is the group of teachers that is out of
step (significantly: $p < \cdot05$); this is of some interest in as much as
these test sentences concern points of prescriptive usage.

The [c] Groups

Compliance tests: None of the 30 tests shows significant variation in
RNC scores.

Evaluation: there were 32 tests; for the plus scores the groups significantly disagree only over one:

N5 $p < \cdot025$

For the minus scores, there was again only one test over which
groups significantly disagreed:

G3 $p < \cdot05$

The [d] Groups

Compliance tests: the groups were in agreement over 28 of the 30
tests, the exceptions being:

D2 $p < \cdot05$
G3 $p < \cdot025$

Evaluation tests: for the plus scores, the groups agree over all 32 tests;
   for the minus scores, they agree over 31, the exception being
   V2 $p < \cdot 01$
   with the presence of small numbers as a distorting factor.

GENERAL COMMENT

The disagreements in results between groups as a whole would clearly
seem to be both sporadic and trivial. The only exception might be perhaps
in the compliance results with the [a] Groups, and even here the number
of disagreements seems to be grossly inflated by the effect of small
scores upon the χ^2 test. We may thus feel some reassurance that the
groups are reasonably representative, and that the sum of their scores
would provide a soundly based sample from which linguistic conclusions
could safely be drawn.

However, a minority of tests give significantly different results as between groups on occasion, and – more especially – as between different
orderings, as we have seen in Chapter 4. Two conclusions seem plain
from this: the first is that we need to have the reactions of several groups

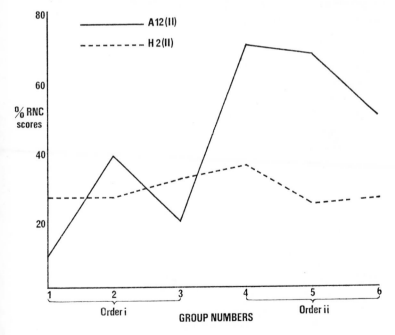

Fig 5: Test and group variability

of subjects for each battery and that the battery needs to be presented in at least two orderings; the second is that results thus obtained are satisfactorily complementary. This can be seen from *Fig* 5, which compares two sets of compliance results for Battery II, the one representing test sentences giving a wide range of results, the other a narrow range.

The figure shows that, while it would not have mattered where experimentation had stopped for H2, the results for A12 varied widely from group to group and – more especially – from Order (i) to Order (ii) and that a conflation of all six results is minimally necessary to offset the group- and order-variation. One might suggest that the plotting of results from a number of groups in this way is necessary in order to distinguish between those sentences for which a conflation provides a reasonable 'final' result and those few (like A12 perhaps) for which still further group results are desirable.

SUBJECTS' CONSISTENCY

We turn now to procedures that we have developed in order to find out how consistent an individual was with respect to a given test. Two types of experiment were used. 85 subjects were given the same test (H5) as the seventh and fifty-first item in Battery I (about 18 minutes apart), and were subsequently asked to evaluate twice likewise (about six minutes apart). Similarly 179 subjects were given the same test (F7) as the third and fifty-first item in Battery II and were asked to carry out a repeated evaluation subsequently. It should be noted that no indication was given in either case that test 51 repeated an earlier example; indeed, one group of subjects were questioned closely on this matter and we found no evidence that they had noticed that 51 was a repetition.

The other experiment consisted of repeating a block of ten performance and ten judgment tests after completing a battery of 51 performance and 51 judgment tests (about 30 minutes apart). Thus in this case the repetition comes after the subjects have had a judgment test and overtly know when they begin the repeated operation tests that evaluation is involved in the experiment. Moreover, they are formally told that some of the tests are going to be repeated. This procedure was carried out with 26 subjects repeating the first ten tests in Battery II and with different subjects (n = 38) repeating tests 11–20 of the same battery.

In addition we have incidental evidence on individual consistency after an interval of one week. The first 25 sentences of Battery II were presented to a group of medical students at St Bartholomew's Hospital Medical College, and one week later, the same group of students were faced with the whole battery without our giving them any indication that they had experienced part of it before.

The degree of consistency displayed by subjects in each of the types of repetition experiment is displayed in the accompanying histograms (*Figs 6–9*). These are compounded of each individual's score matched for the two experiences of the particular test sentence. Where there is shading across the two columns, this means that on both occasions individuals to the stated number have RNC scores; an unshaded match across columns means correspondingly that individuals have on both occasions other than RNC scores. The remainder of each column shows where individuals have been 'inconsistent'.

A: *Single sentence repeated at end of battery*

It will be seen from *Fig* 6, that a large majority of subjects in Batteries I and II have been consistent in their responses for tests H5 and F7 respectively. In the case of H5 71/85 subjects obtained identical scores on both occasions; of the remaining 14 subjects, a majority moved towards RNC scores. With F7, one subject made no second response for lack of space; 146/178 subjects obtained identical scores on both occasions; of the remaining 32 subjects, the overwhelming majority moved away from RNC scores. A very high level of consistency is thus shown (84 per cent and 82 per cent respectively) and this gives welcome assurance that subjects' behaviour suffers neither from lack of experience at the outset nor from fatigue at the end of either battery; and that, in general, a response near the beginning of a battery need not be expected to show markedly different results from a response near the end.

After the compliance component ending with the repeated test, the same subjects had an evaluation test on corresponding sentences again including a repeated sentence at the end. With H5 only 4/85 subjects made radical changes (three from acceptance to rejection and one from rejection to acceptance): 95 per cent consistency. With F7, only 19/179 made radical changes (90 per cent consistency), the minority for the most part moving from rejection to acceptance. There are three points to notice here. First, there is a general high level of consistency. Secondly, this may be expected to be higher where the evaluation is relatively more polarised: thus with H5, the average overall results for the two runs are 80 per cent rejections to five per cent acceptances, while with F7 the average overall results are 51 per cent rejections to 20 per cent acceptances. Thirdly, the trends for the inconsistent minority are in contrary directions that are congruent with the minority trends for the compliance tests,

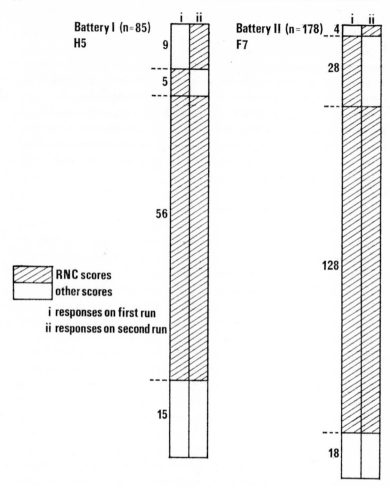

Fig 6: Consistency of individuals

small though these trends may be. With the F7 compliance results the trend is for subjects to move away from RNC scores, leaving sentences with the deviances unchanged on the subjects' second experience of them. This is the kind of trend that we might well expect and it is confirmed, as we shall see below, in the blocks of repeated sentences. With H5, on the other hand, not only is this trend absent but if anything there is a converse trend.

B: *Repeated sequences on the same occasion*

After having had both the performance and evaluation components of Battery II, Order (i), the Group 3 subjects (n=26) were given the first ten sentences for a second performance run, followed immediately by a second evaluation run. The compliance results are compared in the accompanying histograms (*Fig* 7) and it will be seen that with two exceptions there is a high level of consistency similar to that with the single repeated sentences that we have been considering in (A) above. With B10, C3 and L2 we have over 95 per cent consistency in the two runs; with A1 we have 85 per cent consistency and F7 77 per cent. The two exceptions are H11 (69 per cent) and H2 (54 per cent) to which we shall return below. The evaluation results show the same high consistency as with the single repeated sentences, averaging 93 per cent basic consistency for the ten tests.

Sentences 11–20 of Battery II Order (ii) were similarly repeated by the subjects constituting Groups 4 and 5 (n=38). The compliance results are compared in the accompanying histograms (*Fig* 8), again showing high consistency. With C9, F8, M4 and P2 we have over 90 per cent consistency; with Q2 we have 87 per cent consistency, L1 84 per cent, C12 and H10 79 per cent, and A10 76 per cent. The evaluation for these sentences averages 95 per cent basic consistency.

A word may be added on the minority of tests in which a lower consistency in the compliance component has been noted, particularly H11 and H2. In the former, we have in exaggerated form the tendency to decreased RNC scores that we noted with the single repetition, F7, and the histograms show that this tendency is widespread, even where the room for movement is slight. With H2, the pattern is more like that observed with the single repetition, H5, though this time subjects are equally divided between those who move towards RNC scores and those who move in the opposite direction. It will however be observed that the tendency to inconsistency at all is greatest with those tests that show least polarisation as between a high or low number of RNC scores in the first run.

Finally, it should be noted that since the levels of consistency in compliance tests reported in Sections (A) and (B) are similarly high we may reach the interesting conclusion that the intervening evaluation test (which might suggest to subjects the purpose of the compliance test) has not affected their responses. This was strikingly confirmed when two linguists thoroughly acquainted with the technique and purpose of the experiment joined a group of subjects doing Battery I, since their responses

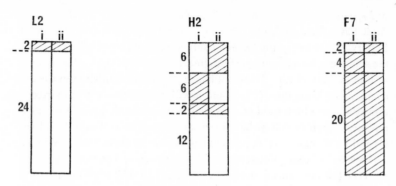

Note: In addition, B10 shows almost complete consistency but having
   only 1 RNC score is not represented diagrammatically. The other
   3 tests from 1–10 are excluded since they are selection or
   completion tests.

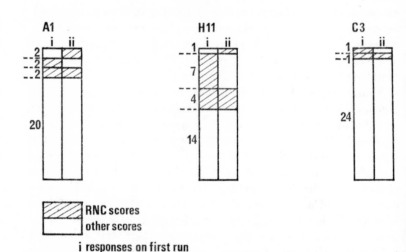

Fig 7: Consistency of individuals: tests in sequence 1–10 repeated
   Battery II compliance tests: Group 3 (n = 26)

were no different from those of the genuinely 'naive' subjects. This has
important implications in the extent that it indicates the possibility of
using the same subjects on more than one occasion for this type of
linguistic testing. Moreover, the expectation of little carry-over effect

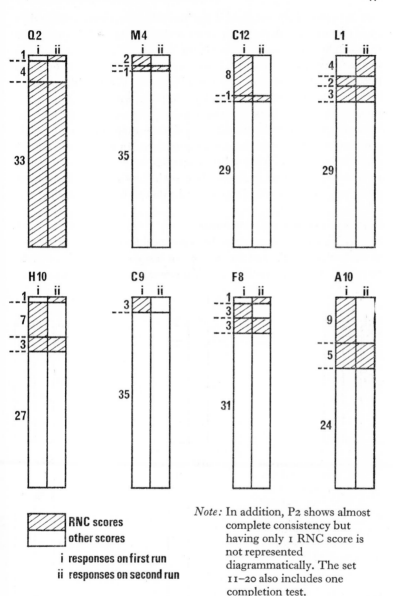

RNC scores
other scores

i responses on first run
ii responses on second run

Note: In addition, P2 shows almost
complete consistency but
having only 1 RNC score is
not represented
diagrammatically. The set
11–20 also includes one
completion test.

Fig 8: Consistency of individuals: tests in sequence 11–20 repeated
Battery II compliance tests: Groups 4 & 5 (n = 38)

48 ELICITATION EXPERIMENTS

may be reassuringly increased if the interval is some weeks rather than some minutes as with the experiments so far mentioned. Of course there may well be two factors involved in the repetition experiments, difficult to disentangle: on the one hand, memory of a specific response (and this may contribute to consistency if the subject was satisfied with his earlier response or to inconsistency if he was not); on the other hand, the accumulated experience of performing a specific task on a specific test sentence (and this may militate against consistency, especially with those test sentences which become deviant on operation). In any case we are not really interested in giving subjects identical tests after an interval of time, but in using them again for a different battery of tests. The evidence of the repeated tests would seem to make this perfectly reasonable.

c: *Repeated sequences after one week*
Brief reference may be made to the experiment (performance tests only) at St Bartholomew's, and the next set of histograms (*Fig* 9) compares responses on the two occasions with reference to the early sentences in

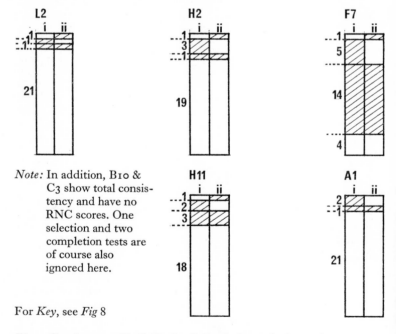

Note: In addition, B10 & C3 show total consistency and have no RNC scores. One selection and two completion tests are of course also ignored here.

For *Key*, see *Fig* 8

Fig 9: Consistency of individuals: St Bartholomew's Group (n = 24) Battery II compliance tests

Battery II Order (i) that we have already considered under short-term repetition in (B) above, *Figs* 7 and 8. It will be seen that a similar high level of consistency obtains and that the dominant trend for such inconsistency as we have is away from RNC scores.

One notable difference between the St Bartholomew's results on both occasions and the Group 3 results on both occasions is the smaller number of RNC scores in general among the St Bartholomew's results. This difference suggested to us that the conditions under which experiments are conducted may have an important effect on results. Whereas in all previous experiments, the subjects were aware that the investigators were from an English Department, at St Bartholomew's the tests were conducted by medical scientists in the course of a series of tests, predominantly psychological. We therefore decided to conduct an experiment exclusively concerned with the effect of differing experimental conditions. This is described in the next chapter.

Chapter 6

The influence of
experimental environment

We have seen (pp 41 f) that, given the obvious variables of order-influence and subject's profession-background, each test has to be carried out with different groups and in more than one ordering before results can be accepted as valid. There are other variables whose influence is still more difficult to estimate and indeed whose very presence is difficult to detect. Do the subjects who are students of English make responses of a particular configuration because they are 'Arts' students or students of English (different aspects of 'profession-background') or because – as students of English in the University of London – they know something of the professional interests of the investigating team? More broadly, does it matter less that the subjects are members of an English Department than that the subjects know the investigators to be so?

The importance of subjects' impression of test purpose was indicated rather dramatically when the group of medical students at St Bartholomew's Hospital were given Battery II (see above, pp 48 f) under rather special circumstances. An ancillary purpose to which our test batteries have been put has been in pharmacological experiments to examine the performance of language tasks when under the influence of psychoactive drugs. In these circumstances, the language test is only one of several tests, psychological and physical; only medical and psychological investigators are present; and there is no occasion, of course, to mention the provenance of the language component in the testing.

That opinions varied widely among subjects as to the purpose of a test battery was already well established (cf QS 15). In work on Battery II, we began to systematise opinion-collecting by asking some groups to jot down after the compliance tests (but before the instructions for the evaluation tests, which to some extent make the purpose overt) what they thought was the object of the experiment. A classification was evolved for the responses so as [a] to distinguish between subjects who thought the tests concerned mental ability and other broadly 'psychological' matters ('Ps' in *Figs* 10 and 11), and those who thought they concerned broadly 'linguistic' ('Lg') matters (including dialect, sentence structure and even spelling), and [b] to distinguish within the latter category those who rightly connected the tasks with acceptability testing ('Acc'). One of the Battery II groups interrogated consisted of graduate teachers on a linguistics course and they took the test in the presence of the authors: 76 per cent of them connected the test with language usage, almost a half of these correctly suggesting linguistic acceptability. The other was the St Bartholomew's groups referred to in the previous paragraph, only 8 per cent of them relating the test to problems of language and none to acceptability. The sharp difference (*cf Fig* 10) accompanied a decidedly lower RNC score by the St Bartholomew's group for several test

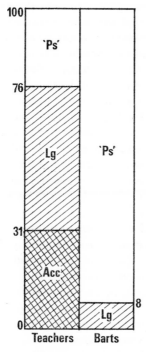

Fig 10: Attitudes to experiment

sentences, as noted on *p* 49, but the strength of the association of these two factors remained uncertain because of other variables in the St Bartholomew's test which need not here concern us. It was suggestive enough, however, to make us look into the matter more closely.

When, therefore, we came to design a test battery specially for experiments in psychopharmacology (Battery IV), we arranged an experiment, in collaboration with Dr J. Svartvik, which would investigate the difference in results that could be attributable to ambience and so at the same time ascertain to some extent what could be offset against mere ambience when the battery came to be used with subjects who had been given psychoactive drugs.

As will be seen from Table 15, Battery IV consists of 25 test sentences ranging widely in both kind and degree of linguistic deviance, as well as in the range of task and the effect of task upon deviance. (*i*) Four of the sentences we could expect to be wholly acceptable both before and after the operation task (1, 3, 5, 21) and were introduced for control purposes. Even so, they range in complexity of task (pronoun change, tense, negation) and of structure (intransitive and ditransitive sentences, and equative sentences with embedded non-finite clause), and the task in 21 is complicated by the possibility of negating either (or both) of the clauses should a subject be confused over the instructions, and the possibility of a semantically equivalent lexical negation (*unkind* beside *not kind*). Five further sentences are predicted to be treated by most subjects as not involving deviance, though alteration or evasion at the putatively deviant point would be scored as 'Relevant Non-Compliance'. Three of these (7, 14 and 16) would retain whatever degree of dubiousness they have irrespective of the particular operation tasks, while two raise a question mark only on operation: 'He used to' (12) confronts subjects with a choice between 'He used not to . . .' and 'He did not use[d] to . . .'; 'She used to' (23) confronts them with a choice between 'Used she to . . .?' and 'Did she use[d] to . . .?'.

(*ii*) A second broad group comprises test sentences predictably unacceptable on presentation and equally unacceptable on performance of the required operation. Two (2 and 11) deal with aspectual problems, the occurrence of 'limited duration' with stative verbs and the perfective with specified past time. In 22, an embedded finite clause has a tag question; the sentence is in any case complex (three clauses) and the task demands two changes. In 9 (again a three-clause sentence) there is deviant embedding involving syntactic blend. In 8 there is deviant selection of a participle where only a nominal (adjective or noun phrase) or finite verb clause would be acceptable. In 13 there is deviant selection of an agential preposition and in addition the sentence has an unrelated reflexive. In 17 there is deviant location of a temporal adjunct and in 6 there is more radical word-order 'scrambling' affecting elements of both phrase and clause structure. The remaining four sentences in this set can be described as semantically deviant. In 4 an inanimate subject has an animate complement and a human-animate verb. In 15, an inanimate singular non-collective subject has a semantically collective or plural verb suggestive of animateness; an adjunct *alone* adds to the deviance by reinforcing both the animate implication of the verb and the singularity of the subject. In 25 a verb requiring a human complement has an inanimate one with an equally nonsensical adjunct of cost-extent. In 19 there are two time adjuncts mutually incongruent, the syntactically dominant one being equally incongruent with the tense of the verb.

(*iii*) Finally, four sentences that were predictably non-deviant on presentation would become seriously deviant if the operation instruction were strictly fulfilled. In 24, subjects could achieve a non-deviant sentence by supplying (unasked and perhaps automatically) secondary concord. In 10, the unspecified change of *any* to *some* would achieve non-deviance, perhaps (though probably not) just as automatically. In 18, 'rectification' would require replacing *last night* by *tonight*, a change that would be easy enough logically but perhaps requiring conscious violation of the instruction. In 20, rectification would require violating the instruction to the extent (scarcely unconscious) of replacing a verb-subject by a subject-verb order.

In all these cases, we scored as RNC those responses that failed to correspond to the target sentence, provided that such failures were directly attributable to the predicted deviances specified above.

The evaluation component of Battery IV need not be discussed in detail. The relation to the performance sentences will for the most part be clear from Table 16, but it may just be noted that (with a view to psychopharmacological experiments) the semantically deviant sentences were replaced in the evaluation test by non-deviant sentences which phonologically echoed, to a greater or lesser degree, the corresponding performance sentences to test the extent to which the former might have a carry-over effect on perception of the latter.

The experiment to compare attitudes to and scores for this battery dependent upon contrasting circumstances of presentation was conducted as follows. A class of English Literature students was without warning confronted by two white-coated persons unknown to them, who

3

announced that they wished to have the students' co-operation in an experiment. The class then allowed itself to be divided in two, one half being immediately conducted from the lecture theatre, the other remaining with the white-coated figures, who issued paper, wheeled in a recorder and merely switched it on. The tape gave instructions for Battery IV and proceeded to elicit a full set of responses for both compliance and evaluation tests; after the last evaluation test, subjects were asked to state 'in a few words' what they thought the experiment had been testing. These students, who were tested under conditions deliberately suggestive of psychomedical science, will be referred to as the 'Sci group'. Meanwhile, the other half of the class had been conducted to the English Department where the authors (who were of course known to the students) met them, issued paper, and playing a copy of the same tape proceeded to elicit a comparable set of results for Battery IV. These students, tested in the familiar environment of the English Department, will be referred to as the 'Eng group'.

It will be recalled that when Battery II was taken by the St Bartholomew's subjects (in conditions similar to the Sci group), the results showed rather fewer RNC scores as compared with other Battery II groups (all of whom had conditions more closely resembling the Eng group). With Battery IV, distinctly more heterogeneous in linguistic character and more varied in test design, one would by no means necessarily expect this difference in result-distribution to be paralleled. Yet, as can be seen by totalling the RNC columns in Table 15, the Sci group had 107 RNC scores beside the Eng group's 129. The difference between Sci and Eng in this respect is the more noteworthy in that [a] 18 of the 25 tests show agreement between Sci and Eng to within one RNC score, and [b] two of the tests – 6 and 20 – show a converse swing, Sci subjects having two and three more RNC scores respectively. The overall preponderance of RNC scores for Eng thus depends on the results of just five tests and it will be worth looking at these in more detail. Three of them (11, 22 and 19) are from set (*ii*) as described above, and two (10 and 18) are from set (*iii*).

Let us first consider these last two, where the difference between the Eng and Sci results is as follows:

	Eng	Sci
+RNC	27	17
−RNC	13	23
	$(p < .05)$	

While both groups closely agreed in carrying out the unspecified secondary change in 24, predicted as automatic, with 10 and 18 the Sci group appear to have had a greater conscious awareness of the need to obey the instructions strictly, even if the result was a deviant sentence. Looked at from the other angle, it would seem that the Eng group have felt less the need to follow instructions than the desirability to carry out the more obvious changes necessary to effect a good English sentence.

By contrast with set (*iii*) where, beginning with a non-deviant sentence, many subjects in both groups 'defy' the instructions so as to respond with an equally non-deviant sentence, the sentences in set (*ii*) were on the whole left by both groups with the deviance they possessed on presentation. The exceptions are almost solely the three in which the Eng group depart from the instructions with decidedly greater frequency to interfere with the deviant feature of the sentence:

	Eng	Sci
+RNC	31	14
−RNC	29	46

$$(p < \cdot 005)$$

Two of them are the cases of aspectual deviance, 2 and 11, and if we seek a reason why these are among the very few deviant sentences in set (*ii*) with numerous RNC scores from either group, the answer would seem to be that the majority, with few RNC scores, are sentences where it is not merely obvious that they are deviant but where it is obvious that they are deliberately – and sometimes amusingly – deviant. If we compare 'We put in the morning the light off' (17) where no one in either group altered the highly unusual ordering of elements or 'The dog looks barking over there' where there was little short of radical reorganisation that could be done to remove the striking deviance, it seems comprehensible that the deviant aspectual expression in 2 and 11 would strike subjects as pointlessly minor and tempting to remove. It is with these sentences that the greatest tension is apparent between those who seek strict adherence to the instructions (Sci) and those who put a higher premium on well-formed sentences (Eng). For the remaining sentence showing considerably different results as between the groups (19), a comparable explanation seems likely. Of the four 'semantically deviant' sentences in set (*ii*), 19 stands out as involving not merely a crazy world of fictitious relationships (clever bathrooms, cars capable of feeling surprise) but a world of relationships that are impossible to conceive, even as a fairy tale. It would not be unreasonable to expect distinctly fewer RNC scores from a group who, rather than regarding linguistic form as the purpose of the test, thought of the exercise as having a psychological purpose, testing memory or concentration, for example.

That the different conditions under which the two groups experienced the test did in fact stimulate just such different opinions of its purpose was made utterly clear in the explicit comments that subjects were required to make. The opinions are categorised as described earlier in this chapter and the respective percentages for the two groups are set out in *Fig* 11. It will be seen that groups from a homogeneous population can be

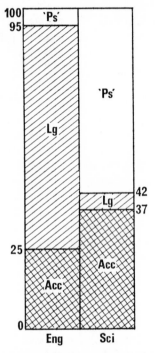

Fig 11: Attitudes to experiment

affected by a few details of 'ambience' so as to render them just as sharply contrasted as the teachers and the St Bartholomew's students (*Fig* 10), two groups of very different backgrounds. And, as we have seen from comparing the RNC scores for the Eng and Sci groups, these opinions are matched – in a rational and predictable way – by differences in test performance. It is thus very important to keep test conditions strictly similar where exactly comparable results are required from groups of subjects.

This is the more important in that ambience is not a straightforward matter of whether or not the subjects know that the test is being presented by linguists in an English department. In *Fig* 10, the teachers were contrasted as a group with the St Bartholomew's students, but this in fact disguises an important and at first sight baffling difference among the teachers themselves that emerged accidentally. One of our principal aims with the teachers (*cf pp 28 ff*) was to test [a] the effect of ten practice sentences, ' +P', before the full battery, [b] the effect of an instruction, ' +E', explicitly stating that only the specified task was to be carried out, and [c] any interdependence there might be between [a] and [b]. The teachers were therefore divided overtly into two groups, one having a practice run before the battery, the other not; and covertly into four groups, so that half of the ' +P' subjects had the explicit instruction while the other half were ' −E', and similarly the ' −P' subjects were half ' +E' and half ' −E'. The number of subjects having a separate 'treatment' in this way was unfortunately small:

+P +E   n=9
+P −E   n=7
−P +E   n=8
−P −E   n=9

Nevertheless, as we examined all the results in relation to ±P and ±E, some were found to contrast with high statistical significance. Thus the comments elicited on the purpose of the test turned out as follows, some subjects thinking the purpose was *both* linguistic and psychological, but most thinking it was the one or the other:

	'Psychological'	'Linguistic'
+P +E	0	9
+P −E	0	7
−P +E	8	2
−P −E	4	7

While ±E cannot be shown to have any importance, the distribution of results in relation to ±P is obviously significant.

	Ps	Lg
+P	0	16
−P	12	9

$(p < \cdot 001)$

Since it seemed incredible that a mere ten additional test sentences (and this is all that ' +P' could mean to the subjects themselves) could account for so sharp a difference in attitude, we searched for other factors. Besides comprising both men and women, the teachers varied considerably in age, length of teaching experience, *etc*, but no isolatable factor corresponded in the slightest to the constitution of the subgroups. We consulted colleagues with experience in educational and psychological research (notably, Mr J. Hall and Dr H. Steinberg) and were advised that one might expect experienced teachers to have a tendency a priori to believe that any questionnaire had a broadly psychological purpose, unless there were something positively suggesting an alternative purpose. With this clue, we looked at the experimental conditions more closely. The half comprising $-P +E$ and $-P -E$ had been tested first, while the other half of the teachers had been taken to a lecture room and given a lecture by a colleague merely with a view to keeping them occupied until they were brought into the room where the experiment was conducted. The lecturer who had kindly co-operated in this had been merely advised to talk to the teachers on anything he thought might interest them. We now found out from him that he had talked about his own research on 'verb + particle' sequences, contrasting the partial mobility of *up* in (say) *They drank up the beer* (beside *They drank the beer up*) with its immobility in (say) *They went up the hill*. The possibility became clear that such a talk on grammar from this point of view could seem to the group, in retrospect as they responded to Battery II, a preliminary to the test itself, this being sufficient to change any a priori notion that its purpose was psychological. The possibility became a probability when we found that among the first ten test sentences (the practice sentences) there was included *They painted blue their fence*, the form of which could hardly fail to remind subjects of the somewhat analogous question of particle-mobility.

We have seen that opinions of the test's purpose can importantly affect RNC scores and that the opinions themselves can be easily affected to a significant degree by small changes in test (and pre-test) conditions. Since one will always want to compare results between batteries and between groups taking the same battery, and since it would be impossible to control conditions (especially pre-test conditions) to the requisite extent, it is vital at least to maintain the practice of seeking each subject's opinion as to the test's purpose so that some degree of 'post-control' is attainable. A more radical possibility would be to achieve parity by frankly announcing the purpose of the battery in advance, but this might well cause more to be lost through sacrifice of spontaneous, 'naive' response than could be gained by similarity of 'ambience'.

Chapter 7

Linguistic problems and scoring criteria

The purpose of this chapter is to set out in summary form the categories of linguistic problem investigated in Batteries I–IIIa, together with the criteria used in operating the scoring system explained in Chapter 3. The contents of the batteries themselves are listed in the Tabular Appendices, where the tests are given in their linguistic category order, the nature of each category being explained below. For Battery IV see *pp 52 f.*

Compliance tests

CATEGORY A

Aim: to ascertain the extent to which certain adverbs differ in their syntactic and semantic function according to whether they are positioned initially in the sentence or immediately before the lexical verb. Sentences were therefore constructed in which the given item appeared in two positions within the same sentence. Though it was expected that there would be stylistic objections to their co-occurrence in any event, it was hypothesised that a greater difference in function between two items in different positions would correlate with a smaller number of RNC scores. Some repeated items were given in two tests, because it was thought that the preverb item varied in function according to the verb with which it was collocated, *viz: honestly believed* (A4) and *honestly reported* (A8) or the subject with which it was collocated, *viz: your father luckily* (A14) and *the game luckily* (A15).

Criteria for RNC: omission or replacement of one or both of the repeated adverbs.

Tests: Battery I: A1-8
       Battery II: A1, A9–14
       Batteries III & IIIa: A15-16

CATEGORY B

Aim: to ascertain the extent to which certain adverbs differ
    semantically. Sentences were constructed containing two adverbs,
    one in initial position and the other before the lexical verb. It was
    hypothesised that a greater semantic difference between two such
    items would correlate with a smaller number of RNC scores. The
    results for this category are intended to be compared with those for
    Category A. To check on some unexpected results in Battery I,
    some sentences were repeated in later Batteries with the omission of
    one adverb, *viz:* B10 and B12 (reduced from B1), and B11 and B13
    (reduced from B4).
Criteria for RNC: omission or replacement of one or both of the
    given adverbs.
Tests: Battery I: B1-8
       Battery II: B9-11
       Batteries III & IIIa: B12-13

CATEGORY C

Aim: to test the acceptability of the collocation of certain degree
    intensifiers with certain verbs and to ascertain whether the
    acceptability varies according to the voice of the verb. For the active
    form, two sentences were given: in one the intensifier was positioned
    before the verb, while in the other it was positioned finally.
Criteria for RNC: omission or replacement of the intensifier or the
    verb; change in the voice of the verb; or change in the position of the
    intensifier.
Tests: Battery I: C1-2, C4-5, C7-8, C10-11
       Battery II: C3, C6, C9, C12

CATEGORY D

Aim: to test the acceptability in preverb position of *badly* and *deeply*
    in various functions of these adverbs, which are determined by their
    collocation with particular verbs. Because the results of Battery III
    suggested that their acceptability in this position was affected by the
    tasks requiring the sentences to be transformed into the interrogative,
    the tests were repeated in Battery IIIa with tasks that left the
    sentences in the declarative form.

Criterion for RNC: failure to retain the given adverb immediately
  before the given verb.
Tests: Batteries III & IIIa: D1-6

CATEGORY E

Aim: to test the relative acceptability of pairs of sentences differing
  only in the position of the adverb: [*a*] in one sentence of the pair
  the adverb is positioned before the verb and in the other it is
  positioned finally; [*b*] in one before the auxiliary and in the other
  between auxiliary and lexical verb; [*c*] in one immediately after the
  verb and in the other finally.
Criterion for RNC: failure to retain the given adverb in the given
  position.
Tests: Battery I: E1-14

CATEGORY F

Aim: to ascertain the frequency with which a given adverb presented
  in the test sentence between auxiliary and lexical verb is
  positioned immediately after the negative particle when the task
  requires the negative transformation of the sentence. A subset
  F10-12 deals with *always*, and it will be observed that contrasts of
  intonation and auxiliary are introduced. In Battery IIIa, F11 and
  F12 are presented in the negative form with the adverb following
  the negative particle.
Criterion for RNC: failure to retain the given adverb immediately
  after the negative particle.
Tests: Battery I: F1-4
       Battery II: F5-9
       Batteries III & IIIa: F10-12

CATEGORY G

Aim: to test the acceptability of a given adverb in initial position in a
  negative sentence or its retention in initial position when the sentence
  is negated. *Suddenly* appeared in both G1 and G2, but with different
  verb auxiliaries.
Criteria for RNC: failure to retain the adverb in initial position or to
  respond with a negative sentence.
Tests: Batteries III & IIIa: G1-4

CATEGORY H

[*a*] *Aim:* to ascertain the frequency with which a given adverb is
  retained in initial position when the declarative sentence in which
  it appears is transformed into an interrogative sentence.

Criteria for RNC: failure to retain the adverb in initial position
  or to respond with an interrogative sentence.
Tests: Battery I: H1, H4-5, H7, H9, H14-16
      Battery II: H2
[*b*] *Aim:* to ascertain the frequency with which a given adverb is
  retained within the sentence when the task requires the
  interrogative transformation of the sentence. In Battery IIIa, H11 is
  presented in the interrogative form.
Criteria for RNC: failure to retain the given adverb or to respond
  with an interrogative sentence.
Tests: Battery II: H6, H10-13
      Batteries III & IIIa: H8, H11

CATEGORY I

Aim: to test the experimental technique by ascertaining whether
  RNC scores correlate with deviance in the test sentence or in the
  target sentence. Deviant test sentences were given with a task
  that would remove the deviance. A low RNC score would
  support the contention that such scores relate to the deviance of
  the target sentence. In the particular test sentences employed for
  this purpose, the deviance arises from the use of *yet* and *at all* in
  declarative affirmative sentences.
Criterion for RNC: failure to retain *yet* or *at all* or to respond with
  the negative or interrogative sentence required by the task.
Tests: Batteries III & IIIa: I1-2

CATEGORY J

Aim: to test the relative acceptability in initial position in the
  sentence of prepositional phrases introduced by *except* and *except for*
Criterion for RNC: failure to retain the given preposition in initial
  position.
Tests: Battery II: J1-2

CATEGORY K

Aim: to test the relative acceptability of *due to* and *because of* as
  prepositions.
Criterion for RNC: failure to retain the given prepositions.
Tests: Battery II: K1-2

CATEGORY L

Aim: to test the relative acceptability of *between you and I* as locative
  adverbial and as 'style disjunct' with the meaning 'confidentially'.

Because it was thought that the position of the phrase at the end of the sentence might have affected the result in L2, the test was repeated as L3 with the phrase positioned initially.

Criteria for RNC: failure to retain *between you and I* in its given form or in its given position.

Tests: Battery II: L1-2
        Batteries III & IIIa: L3

CATEGORY M

Aim: to test the relative acceptability of four types of participle constructions with deleted subject not recoverable from the superordinate clause.

Criteria for RNC: failure to retain the participle construction; or insertion of an appropriate subject.

Tests: Battery II: M1-M4

CATEGORY N

Aim: to test the acceptability of a given number for the present tense of the verb in sentences in which there is conjoining within the subject. In two of the tests (N3 and N4), an adverb is present within the conjoined phrase.

Criteria for RNC: failure to retain the conjoining or (if present) the adverb within the conjoined phrase; or change in the number for the verb.

Tests: Battery IIIa: N3-4, N6-7

CATEGORY O

Aim: to test the acceptability of a given number for the present tense of the verb. O2 is intended to demonstrate the conflict between grammar and logic in number concord. The four other tests constitute two pairs of tests, one having *each* as head of the subject and the other *none*. Within each pair, the sentences differ according to whether the modifying prepositional phrase with plural noun as complement is preposed or postposed.

Criteria for RNC: failure to retain the form of the subject or the number of the verb.

Tests: Battery IIIa: O2-6

CATEGORY P

Aim: to test whether the negative particle is retained in the clause to which it has been assigned in the test sentence. The results should be compared with those for selection tests P1 and P3.

Criterion for RNC: omission of the negative particle from the clause in which it appears in the test sentence.
Tests: Battery II: P2, P4

CATEGORY Q

Aim: to test the acceptability of a sentence consisting of two interrogative clauses conjoined by *but*. In Q1 the subjects of the two clauses have identical reference, whereas in Q2 the subjects of the two clauses are different.
Criteria for RNC: failure to retain *but* between two interrogative clauses; or (for Q2) a change that makes the subjects of the two clauses referentially identical.
Tests: Battery II: Q1-2

CATEGORY R

Aim: to test the relative acceptability of the genitive forms of pronoun and noun when they are in subject relation to a following participle construction.
Criteria for RNC: failure to retain the genitive form or the participle.
Tests: Battery II: R1-2

CATEGORY S

Aim: to test the acceptability of *whose* when its antecedent is an inanimate noun.
Criteria for RNC: failure to retain *whose* or an inanimate noun as its antecedent.
Tests: Batteries III & IIIa: S1

CATEGORY T

Aim: to test the acceptability of the collocation *perfectly good enough*.
Criterion for RNC: failure to retain *perfectly good enough*.
Tests: Batteries III & IIIa: T1

CATEGORY U

Aim: to test the comparative acceptability of a parenthetic clause in a restrictive relative clause according to whether it is inserted immediately after the relative *who* or medially.
Criterion for RNC: failure to retain the parenthesis in the given position.
Tests: Batteries III & IIIa: U1-2

CATEGORY V

Aim: to test the relative acceptability of a subjectless, passive comparative clause according to whether or not another clause is embedded in it.

Criteria for RNC: omission of the comparative clause or (if given) the embedded clause; insertion of a subject in the comparative clause; or change in the syntactic relationship between the clauses.

Tests: Batteries III & IIIa: V1-2

CATEGORY X

Aim: to test the acceptability of -*t* spelling for the inflection of the verbs *spoil* and *smell* in the preterite and in the past participle. The preterite of *smell* appears in two tests, once in the 'receptive' sense (X3) and once in the 'stative' sense (X4).

Criterion for RNC: failure to produce the -*t* spelling in responses that retained the given preterite or past participle forms.

Tests: Battery IIIa: X1-5

CATEGORY Y

Aim: to test the acceptability of the use of *both . . . but* as correlatives with comparative adjectives.

Criteria for RNC: failure to retain the comparative adjectives; or omission of *both* or *but*.

Tests: Batteries III & IIIa: Y1

CATEGORY Z

Aim: to test the acceptability of the subjective form of a pronoun functioning as direct object when it is initial and is contrasted with the subject of the previous clause.

Criteria for RNC: failure to retain the pronoun in the subjective form or objective function.

Tests: Batteries III & IIIa: Z1

Selection tests

CATEGORY N

Aim: to ascertain whether a singular or plural verb is selected more often in sentences in which there is conjoining within the subject. In three tests (N2-4), an adverb is present within the conjoined phrase.

Valid responses (*cf pp* 23 *f*) retain the conjoining, the adverb (if given) within the conjoined phrase, and the present tense of the verb.

Tests: Battery II: N1-2
       Battery III: N3-7
       Battery IIIa: N5

CATEGORY O

Aim: to investigate the preference for a singular or plural verb where
    the concord problem is not related to conjoining. O1-2 are intended
    to demonstrate the conflict between grammar and logic. The four
    other tests constitute two pairs, one having *each* as head of the
    subject and the other *none*. Within each pair, the sentences differ
    according to whether the modifying prepositional phrase with plural
    noun as complement is preposed or postposed.
Valid responses retain the subject in the form given and the present
    tense of the verb.
Tests: Battery III: O1-6
       Battery IIIa: O1

CATEGORY X

Aim: to ascertain whether the *-t* or the *-ed* spelling of the inflection of
    verbs *spoil* and *smell* is selected more often in the preterite and in
    the past participle. The verb *smell* appears in two tests, once in the
    'receptive' sense (X3) and once in the 'stative' sense (X4).
Valid responses contain the preterite or past participle, as required.
Tests: Battery III: X1-5

Chapter 8

Linguistic problems and experimental variation

Compliance tests provide us with a tool for demonstrating the extent to which two items may be classed together. But this need not be merely a matter of whether the items in analogous constructions produce a similar number of RNCs. We may be interested, rather, in the details of the changes that subjects make in the course of responding. For example, the two following test sentences, requiring the same operation task (negation)

1. She has wisely refused your offer. (F5)
2. He has kindly accepted our invitation. (F6)

produced a similar number of RNCs. But the important aspect of the result was not this but the fact that with *wisely* the RNCs relate chiefly to transposition, whereas with *kindly* they relate to omission, transposition and replacement. Thus, irrespective of the *number* of RNCs, the *details* of the RNCs show the different grammatical relations of these two adverbs. Despite the superficial identity of the semantic relation between each adverb and the rest of the clause in (1) and (2), as might be supported by the reasonable paraphrases

1a. She was wise to refuse your offer.
2a. He was kind to accept our invitation.

we see that at least in the negative form of the clauses the semantic relation is different and that an analogous difference may be being masked in the declarative forms; this is supported by the different privileges of position:

1b. Wisely, she has refused your offer.
2b. *Kindly, he has accepted our invitation.

By contrast, we were able to show that *strangely* and *surprisingly* appear
to have a similar relation to the clauses in which they operate, and that
their similarity to each other is not disturbed by an interrogative transformation in which they both have a changed relationship to the clause.

Particular operations may obviously, therefore, reveal distinctions that
other operations will not. We decided to do a full-scale experiment, by
re-testing most of the test sentences in III with a sharply changed set of
operation tasks. We were further motivated to tackle this in order to
investigate the extent to which the putative difficulty of a task affects the
degree of compliance or types of non-compliance. From this comparison
indeed, we hoped to be in a position to offer postulations about the depth
of reorganisation involved in different grammatical operations.

The modified battery (which we refer to as IIIa) was presented to a
large group of subjects (Group F, n = 70) and the test sentences were in
the same sequence as for Groups D and E, *ie* Order (i), n = 55. There was
no judgment component and we have only compliance and selection
tests to consider. Of these, six compliance and two selection tests were
left with the tasks and test sentences unchanged, thus providing a basis
for establishing general consistency between Group F and the groups
earlier tested with the original Battery III. The results are as follows.

A : Sentences with unchanged task

I. COMPLIANCE TESTS

	RNC	non-RNC	
A15	42	13	(Groups D and E)
	43	27	(Group F)
F10	42	13	
	55	15	
H8	30	25	
	31	39	
I1	0	55	
	1	69	
U1	4	51	
	11	59	
Z1	20	35	
	25	45	

2. SELECTION TESTS

	sg	pl
N5	3	45
	11	54
O1	50	5
	62	7

No variation in the above scores is statistically significant and we therefore note the important fact that, where conditions are comparable,
Group F behaves in ways that are to all intents and purposes identical
with Groups D and E. We may therefore conclude that, in such other
tests as show a significantly different result, the variation is attributable
unequivocally to the task variation.

B : Sentences with changed task fall into the following groups

I. COMPLIANCE TESTS

[a] those in which the task was irrelevant to the presence or absence of
deviance in the test sentence and in which consequently only the task
was changed; for example,

/sŭddenly# the /man wouldn't move the car any fùrther# (G2)

original task: *the man → he*
new task: *the man → the men*

[b] a single example in which a deviance was removed by the original task
and where a new task has been devised which would similarly remove
it:

she has /mentioned it at àll# (I2)

original task: → question
new task: → negative

[c] those in which the original task introduced a deviance and where,
with the new task, it was necessary to emend the sentence to become
deviant on presentation in order to achieve comparability. For example, the original test (F11)

they could /always go there tomòrrow#   → negative

was replaced by

they /couldn't always go there tomòrrow# *tomorrow → this afternoon*

[d] those in which the original task introduced an unsuspected problem which was not so introduced by the new task. For example,

he /badly needed the mòney# (D1)

original task: → question
new task: *he → they*

[e] those in which the original task was irrelevant and where the new task introduced an unsuspected problem. For example,

be/tween you and Ǐ# she's /very clèver# (L3)

original task: → negative
new task: → question

2. SELECTION TESTS which, with new tasks, became compliance tests. In these cases, one of the selection forms was introduced into the test sentence; for example, in place of the original test (X1)

they have /ruined my hòliday#   *ruin → spoil*

we gave one of the common selection forms, *spoilt*, in the test sentence:

they have /spoilt my hòliday#   → negative

In some cases it seemed desirable to introduce additional changes of a minor kind, as when *tonight* was replaced by *last night* to give a slightly more plausible sentence.

We have seen that where the tasks remained unchanged, the results showed no significant difference. With the 38 sentences with changed tasks, we find 15 that produce results that are also not significantly different. Eight of these are in the [a] group above; there is one in each of the groups [b], [d] and [e]: and four are among the former selection tests.

		RCN	non-RNC	
[a]	A16	11	44	tense (original task: Groups D and E)
		23	47	replacement and concord (new task: Group F)
	B12	0	55	tense
		6	64	negation
	B13	0	55	tense
		0	70	question
	G1	3	52	negation
		6	64	tense

		RNC	non-RNC	
	G2	0	55	pronominalisation
		1	69	number
	S1	3	52	replacement and concord
		2	68	tense
	T1	0	55	number
		1	69	tense
	Y1	42	13	pronominalisation
		52	18	replacement and concord
[b]	I2	0	55	question
		2	68	negation
[d]	D3	39	16	question
		46	24	tense
[e]	V2	27	28	pronominalisation
		34	36	negation: first verb only

FORMER SELECTION TESTS

	sg	pl	
N4	26	6	tense (for selection)
	32	6	question (plural given)
N6	43	11	tense (for selection)
	9	3	question (plural given)
O2	5	48	tense (for selection)
	5	54	question (singular given)

	-ed	-t	
X3	17	37	tense (for selection)
	4	14	replacement (-t given)

The eight in group [a] should cause no surprise; they provide reassurance on the reliability of the test technique. Since we have wanted task variation within each battery so as to avoid habituation, it is good to have this assurance that, where tasks are not relevant to a deviance, it makes little difference which task is required. This is true with tasks as disparate as question and tense. It is true with sentences that are totally non-deviant, as B13

Mrs Smith totally rejected his gift.

or very deviant, as Y1

Alice is both older but happier than she was.

And it is true with sentences of very different deviance type, as we see from the scatter of test category labels in the foregoing list.

Much of what has been said applies also to the single instance of [b] group in the changed-task material: I2, cited above (p 69). In this instance, however, the point is not that the tasks are equally irrelevant but that they are equally relevant; in both cases, they cause the deviance in the test sentence to disappear.

As we shall see, it is exceptional for test sentences in task-variation groups [d] and [e], as well as for former selection-test sentences, to give closely similar results in the changed circumstances. The particular exceptions we have here, however, are understandable enough. In the case of D3

they /badly treated the sèrvant#

the deviance is sufficiently great in the declarative form for the interrogative not to increase the deviance significantly (see further below, p 79). With V2

the /man has a smaller salary than was thòught he had#

although the new task (negation) increases the deviance somewhat, it also increases the difficulty of rectification. Thus, for example, in III, subjects were able to rectify with a fairly simple insertion of *it* as an RNC:

He has a smaller salary than *it* was thought he had.

With the negative form, such insertion improves the sentence little if any:

He hasn't a smaller salary than it was thought he had.

and subjects achieving a rectification were obliged to offer a sentence with a more radical change such as

He hasn't as small a salary as was thought he had.

We shall leave the discussion of the former selection tests which, exceptionally, yield similar results until we discuss the contrasting results below.

With 23 of the 38 sentences with changed operation task, we found results to be significantly different as follows. We give the test items below in their task-change groups:

		RNC	non-RNC	
[a]	U2	32	23	pronominalisation (Groups D and E)
		57	13	tense: three verbs (Group F)
		$p < \cdot 01$		
[c]	F11	36	19	negation
		7	63	replacement
		$p < \cdot 001$		
	F12	35	20	negation
		1	69	replacement
		$p < \cdot 001$		
	G3	20	35	negation
		1	69	tense
		$p < \cdot 001$		
	G4	21	34	negation
		9	61	tense
		$p < \cdot 005$		
	H11	15	40	question
		4	66	replacement
		$p < \cdot 005$		
[d]	D1	26	29	question
		0	70	replacement
		$p < \cdot 001$		
	D2	33	22	question
		15	55	tense
		$p < \cdot 001$		
	D4	18	37	question
		6	64	tense
		$p < \cdot 005$		
	D5	42	13	question
		38	32	tense
		$p < \cdot 025$		

	RNC	non-RNC	
D6	47	8	question
	47	23	tense

$p < \cdot 05$

[e]	L3	7	48	negation
		23	47	question

$p < \cdot 05$

V1	0	55	pronominalisation
	17	53	negation

$p < \cdot 001$

FORMER SELECTION TESTS

	sg	pl	
N3	14	40	tense (for selection)
	56	8	question (sg given)

$p < \cdot 001$

N7	12	41	tense (for selection)
	39	23	question (sg given)

$p < \cdot 001$

O3	50	4	tense (for selection)
	34	29	question (pl given)

$p < \cdot 001$

O4	51	3	tense (for selection)
	29	25	replacement (pl given)

$p < \cdot 001$

O5	36	18	tense (for selection)
	7	22	question (pl given)

$p < \cdot 001$

O6	32	21	tense (for selection)
	15	44	replacement (pl given)

$p < \cdot 001$

	-ed	-t	
X1	20	35	replacement (for selection)
	6	63	negation (-t given)

$p < \cdot 001$

	-ed	*-t*	
X2	28	24	tense (for selection)
	5	65	replacement (*-t* given)

$p < \cdot 001$

	-ed	*-t*	
X4	19	36	tense (for selection)
	8	62	pronominalisation (*-t* given)

$p < \cdot 005$

	-ed	*-t*	
X5	22	32	replacement (for selection)
	10	59	negation (*-t* given)

$p < \cdot 005$

We may begin discussion of these results with a consideration of the former selection tests as a whole. The test category N investigates the choice of singular or plural verb forms with singular noun phrases as subject linked by

N4   as well as occasionally
N6   in addition to
N3   and therefore

With the original selection task, singular was selected predominantly with N4 and N6, plural with N3. In Battery IIIa the minority form of verb in each case confronted subjects with an interrogative operation task. The revised N4 and N6 tests confirmed the earlier results since subjects chose to alter to a singular form more often than they retained the given plural form. With the revised N3, however, a very different result emerged, showing that the singular verb, which had been a minority form in the selection test when the verb was following the linked noun phrases, was retained by an overwhelming majority of subjects now that the verb preceded these noun phrases:

Is Mr Jones and therefore his son resigning from the party?

Since the singular verb in the declarative form of N3 was rejected much more decisively in the Battery III evaluation than were singular verbs in N4 and N6, we may assume that the difference between the N3 results in III and IIIa must be attributed to the reduced strength of the concord tie when the concord-bearing verb-form precedes the subject, as in a question. It should be added that the concord tie is already weakened by the interposition of *therefore*: even in the declarative order used in the selection test 14/54 subjects selected the singular verb. We may compare the results of N1 (II) and N2 (II) where for *Mary and William sometimes* a plural verb was universally selected while for *John and sometimes Harry* a singular verb was selected by 17/134 subjects.

The test-category O also concerns singular/plural concord in the verb. O2 deals with the degree to which there is conflict between logic and grammatical concord in the selection of a verb form whose subject is the logically singular *fewer than two students*. A grammatical plural is favoured almost universally, and this is shown equally in the selection version of the test and in the revised compliance version (in which indeed the singular form was given, whereupon subjects replaced it by the plural). Moreover, in the Battery III preference test, where the same sentence appeared in the two forms for rating and ranking, the plural form was not merely overwhelmingly preferred but was the only one to be rated as acceptable.

N7 was intended to be a logical test, investigating the concord dictated by noun phrases having co-ordinate premodifiers contrasting as follows:

A black and a white dress ($= 2$ dresses)
A black and white dress ($= 1$ dress)

It was expected that the sequence *Pure and impure love* would be interpreted as structurally similar to the first of these. The selection test bore this out in a large majority of cases, and it was further confirmed by the preference test, though more equivocally, the singular verb appearing to be acceptable to more than a third of the subjects (more than a half with two groups). In the IIIa revision, however, a compliance test with the singular form given shows a decided majority favouring this singular usage, and the contrast between the III and IIIa results is significant ($p < \cdot 001$). This is no doubt largely attributable to the same factor as was adduced for N3 above; the IIIa version is alone in having the structure involved in a question with the presumably reduced strength of concord tie that results. It should be noted however that even in the other tests directed at this problem a considerable minority favour the singular form – notably seen in the preference test – and allowance must be made for an ambiguity in the structure which allows subjects to conceive of a love that can be simultaneously pure and impure.

The remaining concord tests deal with the concord dictated by subject phrases having a formally singular head (*none, each*) and a plural modifier:

O3   each of the children
O5   none of the children
O4   of twenty reviewers, each
O6   of thirty critics, none

The selection test shows the singular verb to be overwhelming for O3 and O4, and this is confirmed solidly by the preference test. In IIIa, the new compliance tests produce significantly different results ($p <$ ·oo1 in both cases) from the earlier tests, the singular form now being only in a narrow majority replacing the plural form that was given. The contrast in results is doubtless to be explained by the difference already postulated between potential and habitual behaviour (*cf pp* 1 *ff*): even though subjects may never initiate a plural concord with *each*, they can apparently find it possible to use such a concord when it is already present in someone else's sentence which they are merely called upon to modify.

A clearer case of this can be seen with O5 and O6. In the preference tests a very large majority of subjects (roughly 3:1) prefer the singular form: this no doubt corresponds to a 'preceptive' attitude sustained by the education system. In the selection tests the singular form is still in a clear majority but its predominance is much smaller (O5 – 2:1; O6 – 3:2). Between this and the revised compliance tests of IIIa there is a significant swing towards the plural ($p <$ ·oo1 in both cases), the form given in the test sentences which is now retained as the majority form (3:1 in both cases).

Tests X1 and X2 deal with variant forms of the past participle and preterite of the verb *spoil*. The results are a classic demonstration of a situation in which a high degree of divided usage seems to exist, with some suggestion of free variation. In the preference tests, about 60 per cent of subjects rated each of the two forms as fully acceptable. A similar proportion ranked each of the two as their 'first choice' (*ie* the preferred or equally ranked form), and this must mean that some subjects gave an equal ranking to both forms, implying free variation. In the selection test, usage was evenly divided as regards the preterite, while for the past participle there emerged something of a bias in favour of the -*t* form. In the compliance tests of IIIa, where the -*t* form was present in the test sentences, the tendency towards tolerance in 'attitude' that we noted in the preference tests seems to have resulted in the retention of the -*t* forms to an overwhelming extent.

Tests X3, X4 and X5 deal with the comparable -*t*/-*ed* variants in the verb *smell*: X3 and X4 are concerned with the preterite of the transitive and intransitive uses of *smell* respectively, while X5 is concerned with the past participle of the transitive. The preference tests show subjects biased in favour of -*t* forms in all cases, but about half were prepared to accept the -*ed* form and a third gave it as their 'first choice'. In the selection tests, it is not surprising therefore that one third of the subjects wrote the -*ed* form, though again leaving -*t* in a comfortable majority. The divided usage is confirmed in the IIIa compliance tests, where again the -*t* forms present in the test sentences were overwhelmingly retained, though in the case of X3 there were so many irrelevant responses that the consequently small numbers do not provide evidence for significance in the χ^2 test.

We come now to the compliance tests with changed tasks which show significantly different results as between III and IIIa (see *pp* 73 *f*). We noted earlier that changes classed as group [*a*] (*pp* 69 *ff*) generally showed results not significantly different as between III and IIIa. Test U2 is exceptional ($p < \cdot 01$) and the difference seems to be attributable chiefly to the greater complexity of the task (originally pronominalisation of a single noun; in the revision, a tense change in three verbs). It seems likely that the more complex tasks obliged the subjects to analyse the sentence more thoroughly and that in the subsequent re-synthesis it would assume a form more in accord with their own grammatical rules for the production of acceptable sentences. But it is possible that the linguistic problem of the sentences was somewhat changed by the new operation task in ways that would tend in any case to increase RNCs. Not only is parenthetic *I thought* somewhat less familiar than *I think*, but the non-consequential requirement to make *I think* past here, together with the focusing *be*, changes the internal relations of the clauses of the original sentence. That is to say, the mere shift to *past* of

Norman is the one who plays I think frequently.

would be

Norman is the one who *played* I think frequently.

All the test sentences whose IIIa task changes put them in group [*c*] give significantly different results as between III and IIIa, and in all cases we find that the IIIa tests give fewer RNC scores. This is what we might expect, given the group [*c*] conditions (see *p* 69). Subjects are less likely to introduce a deviance on their own initiative, as it were, than merely to retain a deviance already given them. This is not to say that the latter procedure is less informative, since the two procedures test different things and yield different information. For example, in being asked to make negative the sentence (G4)

re/lŭctantly# they in/sisted on his resignàtion#

subjects will naturally be inclined to respond with a negative sentence which preserves the semantic relations of the test sentence as nearly as possible. Whereas, with the revised task (a tense change), they are given a sentence with semantic relations not necessarily the same as those in the original test sentence. The IIIa version

re/lŭctantly# they /don't insist on his resignàtion#

means 'With reluctance, they don't insist', while a natural negation of the original test sentence means 'They insisted without reluctance'.

All but one of the changes that fall into group [d] caused results between III and IIIa to be significantly different. These tests are all concerned with a similar problem, three with the acceptability of *badly*, and three with that of *deeply*, in preverb position. *Badly* in D1 and *deeply* in D4 are degree intensifiers equivalent to 'very much', which we expected to be acceptable preverbally. The other adverbial instances were suspected of being unacceptable preverbally, except for *badly* in D2 which we thought might be somewhat dubious. In fact the question-task in III introduced a complicating factor revealing the unacceptability in a question of all these adverb uses in preverbal position. In the revised test, however, the declarative form was retained for both test and target sentences, and the differences originally hypothesised emerged clearly:

	RNC	non-RNC
D1	0	70
D4	6	64
D2	15	55
D5	38	32
D3	46	24
D6	47	23

But while the greater acceptability of the adverbs preverbally in declarative sentences accounts adequately for the difference in III and IIIa RNCs for D1, D2 and D4, it is hardly enough to account for the difference found with D3, D5 and D6, where the adverbs would not seem to be much less deviant preverbally in declarative than in interrogative sentences. The larger proportion of RNCs in IIIa for these three (statistically significant in D5 and D6 but clear enough in D3 also) would seem to be referable to the task difference. In other words, when subjects (in IIIa) had merely to effect a tense change, they did not have to reorganise the structure of the sentences so deeply as when subjects (in III) applied the question transformation, and so they would not tend to reconstruct the sentences according to their own rules: in other words, proportionately fewer RNCs occurred.

There remains only two tests in which the IIIa results are significantly different from those in III. They are both in group [e]. The first involves a situation rather similar to that in the previous paragraph: an adjunct in a question. The original task for test L3 was negation and, as expected, no subjects moved the adjunct *between you and I* from the initial position in the test sentence. It was thought that the revised task, interrogation, would yield a similar result, but in fact it made the initial position less acceptable, producing 14 transpositions. The difference is statistically significant ($p < \cdot 005$). But transpositions are not the only source of RNCs in this test: the other is the replacement of *I* by *me*. Although the difference is not significant (seven in III, 14 in IIIa), the trend suggests that the question transformation in IIIa caused a deeper reorganisation of the sentence than the negation in III (negation of *be*, hence not involving an auxiliary), and so the sentence presented itself more readily for reformulation.

The remaining test to be discussed is V1. With the original task (pronominalisation) it appeared that the test sentence

the /man has a better job than was thòught#

was non-deviant, as we had supposed. The revised task (negation) yielded in fact a somewhat deviant target sentence, and the IIIa responses faithfully reflect this change ($p < \cdot 001$). *Cf* the discussion of V2 above, *p* 72.

To sum up, we have seen two task-change groups that are of special interest. On the one hand, the group [*a*] examples strongly suggest that in general one operation task will produce the same results as another operation task provided neither produces a target sentence that changes the problem present in the test sentence. On the other hand, the group [*c*] examples powerfully demonstrate that some sentences have a relation between their parts that is sharply altered by certain grammatical operations. In such cases, the results obtained from a compliance test will crucially depend on the type of operation task imposed. Moreover, from several examples in different groups, it would seem that the number of RNC responses for a test involving a deviant sentence can depend upon the operation task, and that this is because some tasks oblige a subject to reorganise a sentence more radically than others do, thus making it more natural for the sentence to take on a form nearer that which accords with the subject's rules for the formation of acceptable sentences. Experiments reported by Miller and McKean (1964) seem to have a bearing on this point. They suggest that more complex linguistic transformations take subjects longer to put into effect (through 'some kind of serial processing') and that the extra time is 'spent largely in semantic rather than syntactic operations'.

Chapter 9

Use and attitude:
the relation between test results

It is an important feature of our experiments that, within each battery, and sometimes across batteries, there are tests exhibiting a similar linguistic problem. At some stage we naturally would wish to compare tests within the same category of a battery component, and eventually all in that category across batteries. For example, tests in Category E relate to the placement of adverbs. Through the compliance tests in this category we hope to learn which are the normal positions for the given adverbs. We are therefore interested in finding out the numbers of subjects retaining the adverb in the position alloted to it in each of the test sentences in Category E of the compliance component. More particularly, we are interested in comparing the results of the pairs of tests in Category E which have minimal contrasts in the test sentences, *eg*:

E13   he /hardly could sit still#   *he → they*
E14   he could /hardly sit still#   *he → they*

With E13 and E14 we need to plot the number of transpositions of *hardly* that appear in the response sentences for each test and the positions to which *hardly* is moved. In this way, we shall be able to determine which position in this type of sentence structure is the more normal for *hardly*. This kind of investigation receives only incidental attention in the present book, since it has been utilised, or will be utilised, in studies integrating the results of the experiments within analyses of particular areas of English.

We turn in this chapter to the relation between the results of corresponding tests in different components of the battery. Such tests are given identical designations and are said to belong to the same set of tests.

For example, analogous to the above compliance test E13 is evaluation test E13, which requires an explicit judgment on a three-point scale of acceptability of *he /hardly could sit still#*. Since behaviour and judgment do not necessarily coincide, we have no right to expect that the total of the most serious non-compliances will coincide even approximately with the total of rejections for the corresponding evaluation test. In fact, for E13 the RNC score and the minus score are just within ten per cent of each other, which seems a sufficiently close result for the present purpose. Two features in particular are taken into account in examining the relation between tests: [*a*] how wide the gap is between scores and [*b*] which score is higher or highest.

Our present concern is with the similarities between totals for tests (as percentages) and not with the consistency of the individual subjects. As was pointed out in QS (56 *f*), subjects who make the most serious non-compliances are not necessarily the same as those who reject the sentence in the evaluation test. Because of possible interactions, statistical tests are not applicable to gross totals representing the responses of a group of the same individuals on two or more occasions. We shall therefore have to be guided by percentage differences in estimating the seriousness of the discrepancy between results.

Four types of correspondence will be investigated: (1) compliance test with evaluation test; (2) similarity test with compliance and evaluation tests; (3) selection test with evaluation test or preference test; (4) rating component with ranking component of preference test, where there is no corresponding selection test.

I. COMPLIANCE TEST WITH EVALUATION TEST

The tests most commonly available for comparison are compliance and evaluation. We should note that in Battery I, test sentences were identical for both the compliance and evaluation components in most cases. In Categories F and H, however, evaluation test sentences were of necessity given in the form of the corresponding compliance target sentence, since the linguistic problem was absent in the compliance test sentence and the deviance appeared only as a result of the task. In other batteries the evaluation test sentence was identical with that for the compliance target sentence, with the exception of a few tests that were closely related to some in Battery I and we therefore retained the earlier arrangement to avoid disturbing the comparison.

For the purpose of the comparison, RNC scores will be used for the compliance tests and minus scores for the evaluation tests. A brief justification is perhaps required for the restriction to these two types of scores. As explained above (*p* 20), an RNC score represents an evasion of the problem which the investigator postulates for the particular test or target sentence. Other non-compliances may also be registered, which either indicate that another problem not specified by the investigator is present in the sentence or that subjects are uneasy about the problem but not sufficiently so to evade it. An instance of the former is likely to manifest itself in a discrepancy between the RNC scores and evaluation minus scores, and we shall have occasion to explain the discrepancy sometimes in this way. Instances indicating the unease of subjects, however, may be regarded as parallel to query responses in the evaluation test. The minus denotes an explicit rejection of the sentence. In that respect it is closest to the RNC, which constitutes a behavioural rejection of what has been specified as the deviance.

Figs 12a and 12b display the RNC and minus results for the three batteries, the tests being arranged in category order. If we look at the larger categories, it is evident that there are often distinct result profiles for either the whole of a category or for subdivisions within it. In *Fig* 12a, for example, tests in Category A generally have a low RNC score with a considerably higher minus score, while in C the two scores are, with some exceptions, low and in close agreement. *Figs* 14a–14d are derived from *Figs* 12a and 12b, the data having been redistributed to achieve a grouping that is determined solely by the similarity of result profiles. There are obvious borderline cases which leave room for different groupings, but nevertheless, for the present purpose, there is an obvious gain in drawing attention to similarities that might otherwise be overlooked. Accordingly, we shall base the analysis on *Figs* 14a–14d.

Our principles in redistributing the data of *Figs* 12a and 12b are summarised in *Fig* 13. This shows that we have made a primary division according as the gap between RNC and minus scores is or is not within 20 per cent. With the narrower gap we divided off those sets which have the lowest scores, *ie* where both scores are between 0–20 per cent. This group [*a*] was further divided into a subgroup of sets having scores 0–10 per cent and a subgroup comprising the remainder; the sets in both subgroups are placed in category order in *Fig* 14a. Sets with higher scores but where the gap between scores is ⩾ 20 per cent (group [*b*]) are presented in *Fig* 14b in ascending order according to whichever of the paired scores is the lower. The sets having a wider gap are again subdivided. In *Fig* 14c we have those where the minus scores are higher than the RNC scores (group [*c*]), while in *Fig* 14d we have those with RNC scores higher than the minus

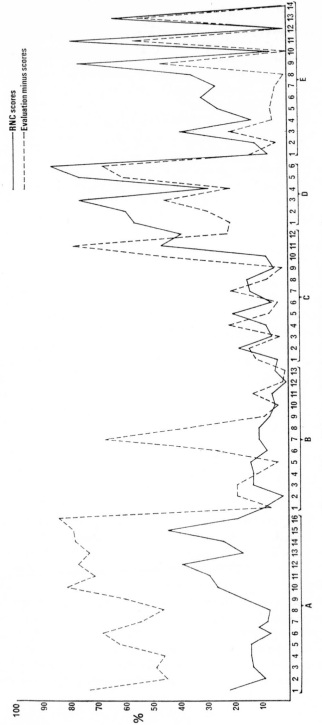

Fig 12a: Compliance and evaluation scores: category order

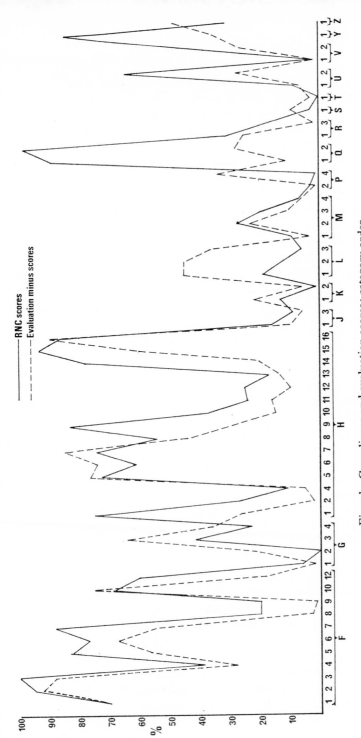

Fig 12b: Compliance and evaluation scores: category order

RNC scores
------- Evaluation minus scores

4

scores (group [*d*]); in both cases the sets are arranged in ascending order with reference solely to RNC scores.

It is noteworthy that of the 116 sets no fewer than 69 (nearly 60 per cent) have a narrow gap, which (as we see from *Figs* 14a and 14b) convincingly demonstrates a close association between the two scores throughout the entire range. Of course the sets presented in *Fig* 14a (40 in all) are largely a negative assurance: we would be alarmed if there were a discrepancy between RNC and minus scores in sentences which we expect to be regarded as non-deviant. Of much greater importance are the 29 sets in *Fig* 14b which display the close association throughout a score range from circa 10 per cent to circa 100 per cent. It is moreover of great interest to see that almost all categories of test are represented in *Figs* 14a and 14b, thus confirming that a close association between RNC and minus is the normal situation.

In *Fig* 14c we have the first of the abnormal situations. It would seem that in this group, where the minus scores regularly run considerably higher than the RNC scores, we have especially those sets which involve an infringement of a semantic kind, typically a lexical co-occurrence rule. It is noteworthy that all 16 of the Category A sets come into this group, and these may be considered together with B7, B8, C10 and C11. Formal specification of semantic relationships (including pleonasm, which we refer to below) is given in Leech 1969, 20 *f*.

Sentences in Category A contain the same adverbial item in two positions, once initially and once before the lexical verb. The sentences in B7 and B8 contain two different lexical items in these positions, *happily*/*fortunately* and *personally*/*myself* respectively. However, their co-occurrence introduces a pleonasm into the sentence, more serious with *happily*/*fortunately* because of their identical syntactic function. It was expected that the greater the difference semantically and/or syntactically between the two items the more acceptable would be their co-occurrence within the same sentence. C10 and C11 are concerned with the collocability of *utterly* and *expect*.

With all these sets, subjects would be required to omit an item or replace it by another item if they were to achieve rectification. Evidently, the deviances in group [*c*] are not sufficiently serious to cause subjects to carry out such a rectification. Pleonasms, stylistic infelicities, and unusual collocations occur in language use, and often they attract little or no attention. On the other hand, when attention is drawn to them, as in the evaluation test, their abnormality is registered. Hence, there is a gross discrepancy between RNC and minus scores in this group.

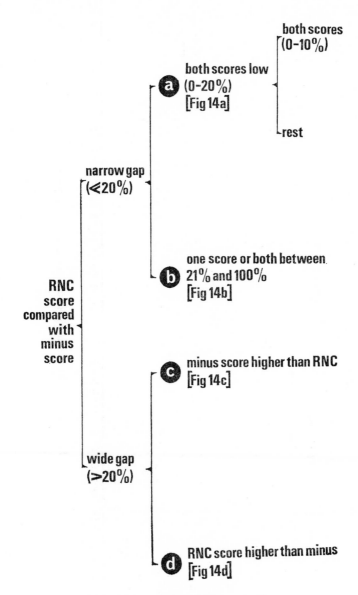

Fig 13: The relation of *Figs* 12 to *Figs* 14

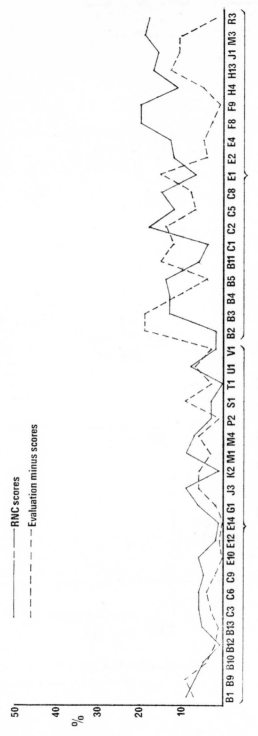

Fig 14a: Compliance and evaluation scores: result profiles

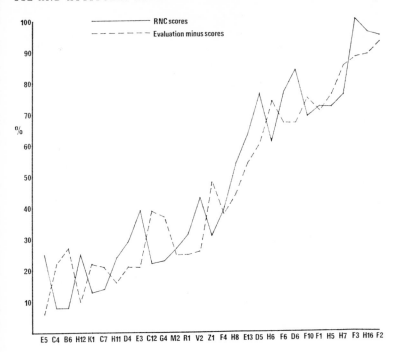

Fig 14b: Compliance and evaluation scores: result profiles

It will be seen that the sets in Category A form for the most part a
smooth upward cline in RNC scores. The gap between RNC and minus
scores, however, shows considerable fluctuation. With two sets, A6 and
A16, the gap is over 60 per cent. So far as A6 is concerned, subjects
agreed, virtually unanimously, that the two sentences with *only* are very
different in meaning (see below, *p* 103). Thus, while there would presumably be a stylistic objection to the repetition of *only* there could be no
objection on the grounds of pleonasm. Why, then, is the minus score so
much higher than with most other Category A sentences? It must be the
case that subjects found grounds for objection additional to those commonly present in Category A sentences. It is difficult to say with certainty
what those grounds might be. It seems not unlikely that subjects reacted
against the initial conjunctive use of *only* (*cf* Greenbaum 1969a, 62) as well
as being affected by the heavy prescriptive doctrine concerning adverbial
only, even though A6 offends against no rule. Given that *only* raises serious question marks concerning its correct usage, it is perhaps inevitable

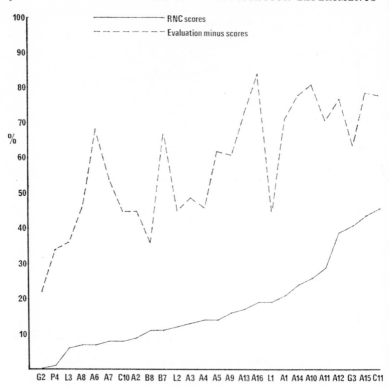

Fig 14c: Compliance and evaluation scores: result profiles

that a sentence containing two instances of *only* should seem unacceptable.

With A16, the problem lay in the double occurrence of the disjunct *surprisingly*, and explanation must involve consideration also of A14 and A15, the other sets which can be interpreted as having disjunct repetitions. In all three cases, the minus scores are very high. In this trio the maverick is A15, which has a smaller gap between RNC and minus scores because it has a considerably higher minus score. This is the result of its appearance near the beginning of the battery for two groups of subjects, as is clear from the sharply different results for the two orders (see *p* 34). These three sets can thus be treated together. As disjunct, *surprisingly* allows only one interpretation, in which it has an underlying relation to the sentence as a whole. Thus, both instances of *surprisingly* in A16, *Surprisingly, your father surprisingly owns a car*, would be inter-

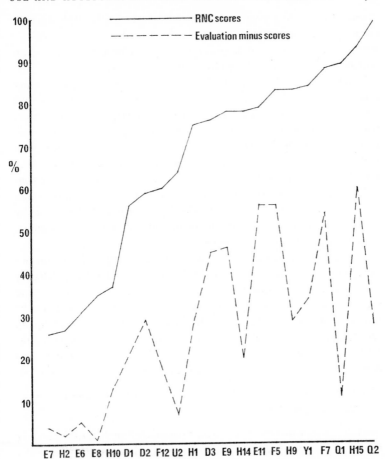

Fig 14d: Compliance and evaluation scores: result profiles

preted as *It is surprising (that)* in relation to the sentence. On the other hand, *luckily* in A14, *Luckily, your father luckily owns a car*, allows two interpretations. Both instances could be similarly understood as *It is lucky (that)*, but the second instance could be taken to refer specifically to the subject of the sentence, giving the meaning *Your father is lucky to own a car*. As expected, there was a larger percentage of subjects perceiving the two sentences with *surprisingly* as very similar in meaning than there was for the two sentences with *luckily*. However, if the subject of the sentence is an inanimate noun, as in A15, *Luckily, the game ended luckily at seven*, the second interpretation of *luckily* is no longer available. Indeed, the proportion of subjects agreeing in this case that the two sentences were very similar in meaning was roughly the same as that for the two sentences with *surprisingly* (cf Greenbaum 1969a, 161–3).

While half of the 16 Category A sets have a minus score of over 70 per cent, four (A2–4, A8) are below 50 per cent. The sentences in these four sets contain repeated items whose functions overlap least of all. Initial *really*, *certainly* and *honestly* in A2, A3 and A4 respectively are disjuncts that contrast with the same items positioned before the lexical verb in that they then appear to have an intensifying effect on the verb. Along these lines we distinguish, for example, between the two instances of *honestly* in A4, *Honestly, Mr Jones honestly believed our story*. On the other hand, the second instance of *honestly* in A8, *Honestly, Mr Jones honestly reported our story*, would normally be interpreted as a manner adjunct, paraphrasable by *in an honest manner*.

In contrast to Category A sentences, those in Category B contain two different adverbs, one of them usually the same as an adverb in a Category A sentence. The two adverbs are similarly positioned, one initially and the other before the lexical verb. Sentences in B1–6 were expected to be non-deviant, and indeed all except B6 are in group [*a*]. B6 is in group [*b*], but displays on a reduced scale the result profile of B7 and B8, with a low RNC score and a higher minus score. The two items *frankly* and *honestly* are very different syntactically in the sentence presented in B6:

/frănkly#/ the /workers were honestly answered by the mànager#/
workers → *worker*

Frankly is a style disjunct and can be replaced by *frankly speaking* or *to be frank* without any appreciable semantic effect, while *honestly* is a manner adjunct, paraphrasable by *in an honest manner* (cf Greenbaum 1969a, 81 *ff*). Nevertheless, there is a sufficiently close semantic affinity between them as items for this to be reflected slightly in the minus score. By contrast, B7 and B8 introduce a pleonasm into the sentence, which, as suggested earlier, affects minus scores more than RNC scores.

With C10 and C11 it is not a pleonasm which causes a much higher minus score than RNC score, though a stylistic-semantic factor is again involved in that *utterly* is not merely an intensifier, but an intensifier expressing the speaker's antipathy to what is denoted by the item being intensified. It is difficult to contextualise such an antipathy in relation to *expect*. We should compare additionally C12 in *Fig* 14b which again has a higher minus than RNC score. The reason for C11 being sharply different from the others in respect of both scores is the presence of the additional deviance, namely the abnormal position of *utterly* at the end of the sentence. In the compliance test for C11

the /students expected his arrival ùtterly⫽   → present

this second deviance could be removed easily by transposition of *utterly* to preverb position. Indeed, 33 of the 39 RNC scores for C11 represent transpositions of *utterly* from the unacceptable final position. Otherwise, the RNC scores for C10 and C11 are virtually the same, five and six respectively.

It is also the position of the adverb that is involved with G2 and G3, with a third example, G4 in *Fig* 14b (discussed on *pp* 78*f*) showing a similar profile in having a higher minus than RNC score. In the first place, G2 differs from the others in that the deviance was already in the test sentence rather than appearing only on performance of the task and this as we have seen (*p* 78) regularly leads to fewer RNC scores. This does not, however, account for the much smaller minus score for G2 than for G3. In both an initial *suddenly* appears in a negative sentence concerned with moving a car 'further'. In G2 the negative is carried by the modal *would*, in G3 by the structural device *did*. The considerably greater acceptability of G2 seems to be accounted for by the fact that the *would* auxiliary partially allows for a double predication equivalent to

Suddenly, (1) he wanted (2) not to move the car . . .

or perhaps preferably for a treble predication with the first deleted, equivalent to

Suddenly, (1) he found (2) he didn't want (3) to move . . .

We may compare

Suddenly, he couldn't drive the car.

which derives its relative acceptability from its equivalence to

Suddenly, (1) he found (2) he couldn't drive the car.

whereas the sharp unacceptability of

*Suddenly, he didn't drive the car.

may be related to the non-existence of

*Suddenly, (1) he found (2) he didn't drive the car.

L1, L2 and L3 are concerned with the use of the subjective form of the pronoun in *between you and I*. Since teachers and textbooks often refer explicitly to the use of *I* in this type of phrase as incorrect, we may attribute the discrepancy to the lower tolerance in judgment, under the influence of the prescriptive teaching. Finally, with P4 the gap is due to the presence of another deviance in the sentence that was not included in the criteria for the RNC scores. P4 required in the compliance test the substitution of *I* for *he* in the test sentence:

he /doesn't know she's còming#

The response sentence was scored as RNC if the negative particle was transposed to the second clause. However, there is evidence from the selection test P3 that subjects felt that the negated sentence required a conjunction between the two clauses, preferably *whether* or *if*. Thus, we may suppose that if the insertion of *whether* or *if* in P4 had been scored as RNC, this and the minus score would have been as close as they are for P2 (*Fig* 14a).

In *Fig* 14d we have the obverse abnormal situation, where the RNC score runs consistently higher than the minus score. None of the categories involved appears in *Fig* 14c and it is important to observe that almost all the sets in *Fig* 14d are concerned with the problems of positional deviance.

To deal first with the exceptions, Q1 and Q2 show the largest gap between RNC and minus scores. Since these tests are discussed in detail in Greenbaum 1969b we need say no more than that they constitute a classic example of the distinction to be drawn between the tolerance that subjects show towards sentences and their readiness to use them when the occasion arises. With Q1, the RNC score mostly reflects the replacement of *but* by *and*. The same is true of Y1, which is also in this group. As we indicated above, however, most tests in group [d] are concerned not with replacement but with transposition, and except for U2 (where the deviance resided in the parenthetic *I think*), with transposition of adverbs.

The sentences in Category D relate to the acceptability in preverb position of *badly* and *deeply* in collocation with specific verbs. D1 (*badly need*) and D4 (*deeply admire*) were thought to be non-deviant. However, the task introduced an unsuspected deviance for these two, as well as possibly an additional deviance for some of the others (*cf p* 79). In some instances, the preverb position is certainly less acceptable in a question than in a declarative sentence. With all six sets the resultant minus score is lower than the RNC score, but only with D1, D2 and D3 (all involving *badly*) is the gap more than 20 per cent. The relation between these three is discussed in Greenbaum 1970, 62 *ff*.

Five of the sets in *Fig* 14d are in Category E. E6, E7 and E8 have a very low minus score with a considerably higher RNC score. E5 in *Fig* 14b, which should be discussed together with these three, has a similar profile though the gap is just under 20 per cent. The four sets constitute two pairs, each concerned with the relative acceptability of two positions of an adverb in an otherwise identical sentence. In the evaluation tests there was little difference between the minus scores within each pair of tests, though E5 had 12 queries (14 per cent) against the two (2 per cent) for E6. All four sentences therefore appear to be acceptable, except that the number of queries for E5 indicate there were some reservations about that sentence. However, the sentences judged in the evaluation component were the test sentences of the compliance component. The higher RNC scores probably point to a difference in acceptability between the target sentences of the compliance component and the test sentences of the evaluation component. It seems that the task of negating the sentence in the compliance test introduced a complicating factor in the acceptability of the sentences. Whereas, for example, E8 *She agreed completely* was rejected by only one subject and queried by only one in the evaluation test, in the compliance test for E8 as many as 30 subjects (35 per cent) did not respond with *She did not agree completely* when asked to negate the sentence. We cannot interpret the discrepancy as a difference between the preferred normal position pinpointed in the compliance component and the non-normal position reported on in the evaluation component, since both positions (the only ones available) have a rather similar RNC rate.

A similar explanation probably applies to the smaller discrepancy in E3 (*Fig* 14b). The oddity of the preverb position of *faintly* in *The girl faintly frowned* (contrast E4) is registered in the 21 per cent of minus scores, reinforced by the 27 per cent of queries. However, the unacceptability appears to be increased when the task required in the compliance test is applied, producing the target sentence *The girl faintly frowns*. The collocation of *faintly* with *frown* (and probably also the preverb position of *faintly*) is more likely to occur in the literary variety of English, and in that variety the narrative past tense is far more usual than the present.

While there may well be differences between British and American English at this level of delicacy of analysis, it is instructive to report the results of an informal investigation among American students. Thirty subjects were asked to indicate whether any of a series of ten sentences, presented visually, were 'odd' to them. The sentences, in five pairs, consisted of the test sentences for E3, E5, E6, E7 and E8 (identical in both components) and the target sentences in the compliance component. The sentences are listed below in the order they appeared, together with the number of informants finding them odd (in brackets).

E5   1a: I differ profoundly from him.   (12)
      b: I don't differ profoundly from him.   (14)
E8   2a: She agreed completely.   (0)
      b: She didn't agree completely.   (8)
E3   3a: The girl faintly frowned.   (13)
      b: The girl faintly frowns.   (18)
E6   4a: I differ from him profoundly.   (5)
      b: I don't differ from him profoundly.   (13)
E7   5a: She completely agreed.   (6)
      b: She didn't completely agree.   (5)

The results are not exactly parallel to the Battery I results we have been discussing, but of course the conditions and nature of the tests are different, even apart from differences that may exist between British and American English. Nevertheless, in the three instances where there are the larger differences in the reaction to sentences within the same pair, the results parallel those in Battery I. Thus, the negative forms of E6 and E8 (with *profoundly* and *completely* in final position) are judged distinctly odder than the affirmative forms, and the form of E3 with the present tense is also found to be odder than the form with the past.

The effect of positional deviance is classically illustrated in E9 and E11, which in contrast to E10 and E12 (which are placed in *Fig* 14a with scores indicating their complete acceptability) have high minus scores and even higher RNC scores. The relevant adverbial position is before and after the auxiliary and the results illustrate the ease with which rectification can be achieved. It is curious that E13 with a similar minus score has a considerably lower RNC score (the gap is sufficiently small for this set to be displayed in *Fig* 14b). It is possible that the greater commonness of *hardly* as a preverbal modifier does not make subjects feel so obliged to change its position in the compliance test. Its partial familiarity may be endorsed by expressions like *You never can tell, Scarcely had he entered, Never have I seen.*

While most sets in Category F show close agreement between RNC and minus scores, three differ considerably with the RNC score much higher. The problem in this category is the positioning of the adverb in relation to a negative particle introduced by the operation task. A high RNC score is predictable therefore where a deviant sentence would result from slavish compliance. The only question in F5, F7, F12 is why there is a wide gap between the RNC and the minus scores in these cases. The problem seems to be that though some adverbs have the same relation to a sentence, irrespective of whether it is affirmative or negative, with other adverbs this is not true. While, therefore, with all Category F we are concerned with the different constraints on position of the adverb in affirmative and in negative sentences, with some we are additionally concerned with the plausibility of retaining the same item in passing from negative to affirmative. Asked to negate *I can fortunately understand her message* (F7), subjects, not surprisingly, seemed to prefer *I can't unfortunately . . .* to the target sentence, but presented with the target sentence *I can't fortunately . . .* in the evaluation test showed their dissatisfaction with the sentence (54 per cent minus) without by any means paralleling the implied strength of reaction against the form that we have in the RNC score (88 per cent). F12 is an extreme case in producing disparity between RNC and minus. In the compliance test, subjects were asked to negate a sentence with *always* between auxiliary and lexical verb, the target sentence for which was *You shouldn't always take it before dinner*. However, many responded with *You should never take it before dinner*, preferring a form that is the logical opposite of the test sentence rather than one that is merely the grammatical negative.

Where F was concerned with the affirmative/negative correspondence, Category H is concerned with the relation between declarative sentences (having co-occurring adverbs) and the corresponding interrogative form. Again we are involved with adverbial position (and sometimes with the retention of the adverb) and again, because the problem only emerges on operation, high RNC scores are to be expected in cases where the target sentence, the strictly corresponding interrogative, would be deviant. Since the transposition of an adverb appears to be an easy operation for subjects to perform, the compliance tests indicate the normal preferred position. The evaluation tests, on the other hand, reflect the judgment of the acceptability of the position, irrespective of its status as the normal or the less usual position. Thus, with H14 and H15 the RNC scores are similarly high – 66 (78 per cent) and 79 (94 per cent) respectively – but there is a vast difference between their minus scores, 17 (20 per cent) and 51 (60 per cent) respectively. We may infer that an aspectual adjunct (*cf* Greenbaum 1969a, 163 *ff*) like *musically* in H14 is acceptable to most if it is positioned in front of a question, though that is not its normal position, whereas a temporal adjunct such as *today* in H15 is unacceptable to most in that position. We can therefore distinguish between two non-normal positions: the *marked* position, as with *musically*, and the *abnormal* position, as with *today*. Of course, both markedness and abnormality are gradable. The position in front of a question seems to be slightly more marked for *actually* (H9) than for *musically* (H14). Similarly, the abnormality of this position is less for *today* than for *suddenly* (H16 in *Fig* 14b), whose high minus score is evidence of great abnormality in initial position in a question, proving that the RNC scores are not reflecting an unmarked position (see further Greenbaum 1969a, 242). This is the reason why we must expect to find *strangely* also in *Fig* 14b with a small gap, since this is the extreme instance of abnormality.

Despite the radical steps required to produce a non-deviant response (by omitting or replacing the adverb or even not complying to the extent of retaining the declarative form), the deviance was apparently considered serious enough to justify a large number of RNC scores. Thus, in the compliance test:

/străngely# they re/fuse to pày#   → question

the transposition of *strangely* does not effect much improvement, if any. Hence the seriousness of the deviance induced 40 per cent of the subjects to omit *strangely* and 16 per cent to replace it by another adverb or construction, while only 15 per cent transposed it. On the other hand, with H16

/sŭddenly# he /opened the dòor#   → question

only 4 per cent omitted *suddenly* and none replaced it, while as many as 96 per cent transposed it. With H2 (involving *incidentally*) the RNC score includes a surprising number of transpositions of the adverb, 30 (17 per cent), mostly to final position. Yet, when *incidentally* was positioned finally in the evaluation test H3 /is he the cháirman incidentally# it evoked 7 per cent more rejections and 11 per cent more queries than in H2 inci/dĕntally# /is he the cháirman# showing that subjects preferred the initial position. RNC scores may arise from the restructuring entailed by the interrogative task, which requires a re-ordering of initial constituents, and they do not indicate that the target sentence would of itself be unacceptable.

We may now take a summary view of the abnormal distribution demonstrated in *Fig* 14d. It is clear that the compliance test is more sensitive to a positional deviance than to the other kinds of deviance represented in the batteries, in as much as transposition is easily effected by subjects in their responses. Even something that is unusual to a quite minor extent may have an effect on the RNC score out of all proportion to the acceptability rating. By contrast, the RNC and minus scores may get out of step to a similar but obverse extent (*Fig* 14c) if the deviance were to invite subjects to undertake a more radical reorganisation of the syntactic or semantic structure of the sentence.

During the course of the discussion on the discrepancy between the two types of score, we suggested a number of factors that may be relevant. Some of these relate to the experimenter's role: [a–e].

[a] The task introduced an unsuspected deviance in the target sentence of the compliance component, which was absent in the test sentence of the evaluation component, resulting in a higher RNC score; for example, with E8 there is evidence pointing to lower acceptability of the target sentence

She didn't agree completely.

as compared with the evaluation sentence

She agreed completely.

[b] The sentence included a deviance that was not catered for in the criteria for the RNC score; for example, with P4, *He doesn't know she's coming*, we were interested only in whether the negation would be shifted to the second clause. Many subjects produced a non-compliant response in which a conjunction was inserted between the two clauses. Such a response, however, was not included among the RNC scores, though undoubtedly the deviance was registered in the minus score.

[c] The order in which a compliance test was given affected the result. In A15, with repeated *luckily*, this raised the RNC score, diminishing the gap between the two types of score. With D4, on the other hand, the RNC score appears to have been lowered, though again diminishing the gap.

[d] If the task introduced the deviance, the RNC score was higher than it would be if the deviance was included in the test sentence; for example, with H11 the interrogative task in Battery III led to a higher RNC score than that for the same test in IIIa where the test sentence was in the form of a question. The task in III was relevant to the problem, which related to the acceptability of *probably* in a question.

[e] If the task directly affected the item, even though the resulting target sentence appears to be equally acceptable, the RNC score is higher than the minus score; for example, in H2, with an interrogative task, many subjects transposed the initial *incidentally*, though initial position seems more acceptable than the final position in which some placed it.

The remaining factors relate to the nature of the linguistic problem. Several of these result in an RNC score that is higher than the minus score: [f–j].

[f] The position of an item (in these experiments, almost invariably an adverb) is at issue. Rectifiability of the deviance is obvious and easy, merely requiring the transposition of the item.

(i) The position is acceptable, on the whole, but is the marked position; for example, *musically* in initial position in the sentence *Musically, was the concert a success?* The minus score for this set is 20 per cent and the RNC score is 78 per cent. The compliance test appears to be highly sensitive to the non-normal position.

(ii) The position is abnormal; for example, *today* in H15 *Today, was the museum open?* The minus and RNC scores are respectively 60 per cent and 94 per cent. The abnormality is tolerated to a greater extent in the evaluation component. If, however, the abnormality is sufficiently serious, the gap between the two scores is narrowed; for example, *suddenly* in H16 *Suddenly, did he open the door?* with a minus score of 89 per cent and an RNC score of 96 per cent.

[g] The two forms in question seem to be in free variation, with perhaps some slight preference for one of them; for example, very few subjects (2 per cent) rejected R3 *Did she hate their coming early?*, but more (12 per cent) preferred to substitute *them* for *their* in the compliance test. This factor may also have played a part in the higher RNC score for H2, referred to in [e], and in F8 and F9.

[h] A logical, rather than purely syntactic, interpretation was given to the task; for example, the task of negating the sentence in F12 *You should always take it before dinner* was understood by many as requiring the opposite *You should never take it before dinner*, thereby contributing to the discrepancy between the minus score (12 per cent) and the RNC score (39 per cent).

[i] Rectification of the deviance is obvious and unique, and requires a minimal adjustment; for example, in Y1 *Alice is both older but happier than she was*, the sentence becomes fully acceptable if *and* replaces *but*. This factor is relevant in all previously-stated cases of higher RNC scores.

[j] Elicited behaviour conflicts with attitude: a form avoided in the compliance tests, when subjects are called upon to produce it, is tolerated in the evaluation test, when subjects are asked to pronounce on its acceptability. For example, with Q2 *Did she wash the cup but he refuse to drink from it?* the RNC score is 99 per cent while the minus score is only 28 per cent. A detailed analysis of the responses shows that there was no obvious way of rectifying the deviance arising from the use of *but* to link two questions. Moreover, many of the changes that were

introduced involved a radical restructuring of the sentence, such as the relativisation of one of the clauses. Conflict between behaviour and attitude, needless to say, is a factor that may enter into all the discrepancies with a higher RNC score.

Several factors result in a minus score that is higher than the RNC score: [k–n].

[k] The sentence contains a semantic and/or lexical deviance. In all instances, rectification requires the omission or replacement of an item. The types of deviance are:

(i) pleonasm resulting from the co-occurrence of two identical lexical items; for example, the repetition of *nevertheless* (with virtual, if not complete, syntactic and semantic identity between the two items) in A5 *Nevertheless, some people nevertheless attempted it*;

(ii) pleonasm resulting from the co-occurrence of two different lexical items; for example, the co-occurrence of *happily* and *fortunately* in B7 *Happily, most of them fortunately admired the achievement*;

(iii) semantic incompatibility of two lexical items; for example, *utterly* tends to express not merely intensification but the speaker's disapproval, and this does not seem to be readily evoked by the verb *expect* in C10 *The students utterly expected his arrival*;

(iv) stylistic incompatibility of the co-occurrence of two identical items, though they differ in their syntactic and semantic relation to the sentence; for example, the repetition of *honestly* in A8 *Honestly, Mr Jones honestly reported our story*.

[l] The deviance is one that has traditionally been frowned upon in prescriptive teaching; for example, the use of the subjective form *I* in L2 *She's very clever, between you and I*.

[m] The deviance, even though not explicitly condemned in prescriptive grammar, relates to an area of syntax that has traditionally been part of the teaching of grammar to native speakers of the language; for example, recollection of instruction on pronominal cases may have resulted in a higher minus score for Z1 *His wife is a cat, but he I like*.

[n] The deviance is conspicuous and may therefore have been left unchanged in the compliance test. This factor is particularly important for Battery III, where subjects were explicitly asked not to make corrections of their own. It is a factor that probably enters into all other cases where the minus score is higher (with the possible exception of the collocation problem in [k]). Conspicuous deviances are undoubtedly also found in sets where the RNC score is higher, but its

effect seems to be minimised because of its co-occurrence with one or both of two more potent factors: easy and obvious rectification of the deviance and the introduction of the deviance by the task. Both these tend to inflate the RNC score.

One important aspect of the relation between compliance and evaluation tests has been repeatedly adumbrated in the preceding pages. It is this. The response sentence elicited in a compliance test may or may not be a close approximation to the target sentence. But at least it bears a direct relationship to the test sentence. In short, it is directly a function of the test sentence and the operation task. In the corresponding evaluation test, the sentence presented (the compliance test's target sentence) is judged not merely in contextual isolation: contextual isolation is, after all, common to both types of tests. The important thing is that the sentence judged in the evaluation test need invite no conscious relationship with the test sentence of the compliance component. In other words, *He can possibly drive* plus negative may well yield *Probably he can't drive* in a compliance test, but offered the strict target sentence in an evaluation test subjects will surely give high approval to *He can't possibly drive*. It is important to remember that in this last case subjects are not committed to saying that they approve *He can't possibly drive* as the negative of *He can possibly drive*.

2. SIMILARITY TEST WITH COMPLIANCE AND EVALUATION TESTS

For many of the sets in Categories A and B there are similarity tests that correspond to the compliance and evaluation tests. Categories A and B relate to problems arising from the co-occurrence of two adverbs in the sentence. In A the two adverbs are identical, though they may differ in their relationship to the sentence, while in B they are different items, though they may be similar semantically and/or syntactically. The equals score represents the number of subjects responding with 'very similar in meaning' in their judgment of a pair of sentences. It was hypothesised that if the two sentences are judged to be very similar in meaning, the repeated items must be very similar semantically and syntactically. Thus, if for A5, the sentences

/neverthelĕss# /some people attĕmpted it#
/some people neverthelèss attempted it#

are judged to be very similar in meaning, then we may suppose that *nevertheless* has a similar function in the sentence irrespective of whether it is positioned initially or before the verb. On the other hand, if the two sentences with *only* are generally judged to be very different in meaning (A6) we must assume that subjects recognise that the two instances of *only* have a very different function within the sentence:

/ŏnly# the /students wòrk during the term#
the /students ónly wòrk during the term#

Indeed, this hypothesis was borne out in the results of the similarity test for A5 and A6:

	very similar	somewhere between	very different
A5	53	4	7
A6	1	1	62

We would expect that the degree of semantic similarity of such pairs of sentences would correspond closely to the degree of acceptability of the sentence in which the two items co-occur and that this in turn would be reflected in the RNC and minus scores. Thus, in the similarity test, we can consider the equals score to be directly related to the RNC and minus scores. Since, however, the RNC scores show little fluctuation, not much would be gained by relating them to the similarity and evaluation scores. Instead, *Fig* 15 deals solely with the equals and minus scores, bringing together the percentaged results of the few relevant tests in the three batteries and grouping them in such a way as to facilitate the accompanying discussion. The three groups that emerge are each ranged from left to right in ascending order of magnitude of gap between the two scores. In group [*a*] the gap is 0–20 per cent, while in groups [*b*] and [*c*] the gap is over 20 per cent, group [*b*] having a higher minus score and group [*c*] having a higher equals score.

Group [*a*] comprises 11 of the 24 sets. For these sets the closeness of the gap suggests that the factors relevant to the similarity of the pair of sentences are relevant also to judging the acceptability of the sentence from which we have derived the pair. This is only to be expected for B3, B4, B6 and B9, which were predicted to be non-deviant control sentences, but it is reassuring in cases like A13, B7 and others, where both minus and equals scores are very high.

In group [*b*] all the sets are in Category A, each containing a repeated adverb. The set with the biggest discrepancy (involving repeated *only*) has been discussed in comparing the compliance and evaluation tests. Stylistic factors seem to be responsible in general throughout group [*b*] for the considerably higher level of minus scores. For example, the very

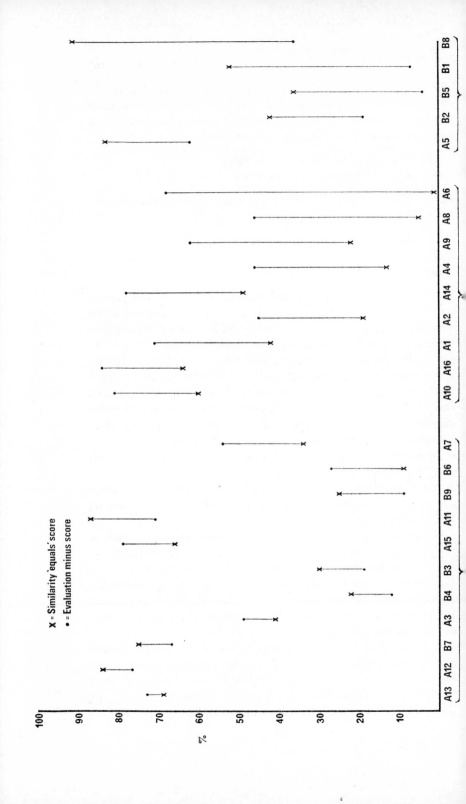

low equals score for A8 is fully expected in view of the quite different relationships of *honestly* in the two sentences:

Honestly, Mr Jones reported our story.
Mr Jones honestly reported our story.

There should therefore be no semantic reason for objecting to the conflation of these sentences as

Honestly, Mr Jones honestly reported our story.

In fact, no fewer than 46 per cent of subjects repudiated the conflated sentence in the evaluation test, doubtless disliking the repetition of the 'same' item despite the unambiguously distinctive usage.

In group [c] there is only one set from Category A (A5) and it is of interest to compare with it the set A11 in group [a] which has similar scores and result profile. These two differ from the remainder of Category A in that the repeated adverbs concerned are conjuncts, *nevertheless* and *therefore* respectively. The high equals score these sentences share is a reflection of the tendency of conjuncts to have only one syntactic function, irrespective of their position. The fact that minus scores are not recorded at such a high level would seem to reflect the not uncommon practice of emphasising concessive and causal conjunction either by correlated items across clauses or by synonymous items in the same clause, for example:

Therefore, for that reason he left.
Nevertheless, he *still* went, *all the same*.

All other sets in group [c] are from Category B, each containing two adverbs with varying degrees of semantic similarity. It is interesting therefore that equals scores are very much higher than minus scores, indicating that the semantic similarity does not provoke a corresponding distaste for the sentence in which the two adverbs co-occur. Thus, the two sentences

Personally, I approved of the idea.
I myself approved of the idea.

were judged to be similar by 91 per cent of the subjects. We might therefore have expected that a conflation of the two sentences

Personally, I myself approved of the idea.

would be rejected as tautologous (and therefore unacceptable) by a similar proportion of the subjects. Precisely this result is seen in A13, to the extreme left of *Fig* 15, where the same sentence (but this time with a repetition of *personally* expounding the tautology) yielded scores with a very small gap between them. With *personally* and *myself* in B8, however, only 36 per cent of the subjects rejected the sentence. Obviously, tautology is less conspicuous when the tautologous items are synonyms than when they are undisguised repetitions. (On the higher equals score for B8, see Greenbaum 1969a, 88.)

3. SELECTION TESTS WITH EVALUATION TESTS

There are six sets with selection and evaluation components to consider and in so doing we ignore omissions and irrelevant responses. We shall regard the plus score for a particular form in the evaluation test as comparable with the score representing the selection of this form in the performance test. All the tests concern number concord, where the subject involves two singular nominals related in a range of structures from simple coordination (N1 *Mary and William*) to the subordination of one to the other (N4 *John as well as occasionally Harry*). Since the singular verb form in each case was that offered to subjects in the evaluation test it is the selection of the singular in the performance test that is adduced for comparison. The results are as follows:

	Selection (%)	Evaluation (%)
N1	0	4
N2	15	38
N3	29	28
N4	85	41
N5	85	56
N6	80	36

In the case of N1 and N3, the selection results closely match the evaluation results. With N1 no comment is necessary, since the unanimity in the one case could hardly co-occur with divided evaluation in the other. With N3 we should compare N2 since the problem involved is rather similar – coordination with an interpolated adverb, *sometimes* in N2 and *therefore* in N3. In both cases it was thought that the interpolated adverb made the second part of the coordination more of a separate predication and that consequently some subjects might consider the first nominal alone as true subject and hence select the singular. But it was predicted that this separation effect would be greater for N3 with the conjunct *therefore* than for N2 with the temporal adjunct *occasionally*. And indeed this was true for the selection test. It was surprising to find the results of the evaluation test going in the opposite direction, but it is fair to point out that the figure of 38 per cent is severely inflated by the responses for groups who in one order had the test early in the battery (see *p* 33).

For N4, N5 and N6 the singular is the predominant form in the selection tests, but this preference for the singular receives only equivocal support in the evaluation test. It would seem that while the singular is thus preferred to the plural, the nature of the concord problem is such that neither the singular nor the plural is regarded by the subjects as winning majority support. Though this seems a plausible explanation of the scores, it must however be borne in mind that we can never be confident that the evaluation test relates in a simple way uniquely to the point that the test designer had in mind. In the present instances it is reasonable to suppose that the low acceptability scores reflect some distaste for the way in which the nominals are organised in the subject expression as well as reflecting concern for the concord problem that arises from it.

4. SELECTION TESTS WITH RATING AND RANKING TESTS

There are twelve sets with selection and preference tests to consider and once again we ignore omissions and irrelevant responses. With the preference test there are two components, rating and ranking. We shall regard the plus score and the ranking score indicating 'first' preference for a particular form as comparable with the score representing the selection of this form in the performance test. The relation between these scores is shown in *Fig* 16. The columns headed 'S' require no explanation since the solid and broken lines simply represent directly the number of subjects selecting the forms indicated. With the other two columns, a slightly more complex situation exists in that it is not uncommon for subjects to express approval (+) or top ranking (1) for both the forms presented in a test. The overlapping scores in *Fig* 16 in these cases thus represent forms which are regarded as being in free variation. We would expect the 'S' column and the '1' column to show close similarity since they are exactly complementary, concerned as they are with the strictly limited choice dictated by the form of the test. With the '+' column, it would be possible to have a somewhat different result since a subject will not necessarily find acceptable either of the forms presented to him. In point of fact, for ten of the twelve sets there is no disagreement between the three scores.

In the case of N7, *Pure and impure love attract(s) the novelists*, while there is a close agreement between the three results it is not easy to deduce a general conclusion with confidence. On the face of it there is a tendency to prefer the plural but those opting for the singular may in

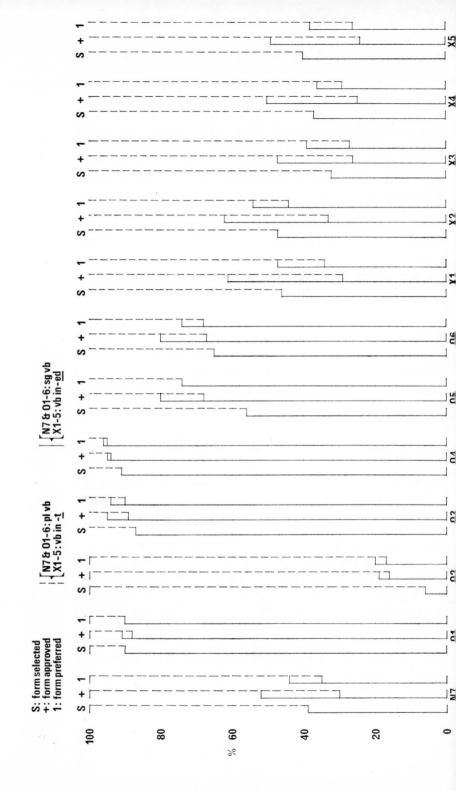

S: form selected
+: form approved
1: form preferred

[N7 & 01-6: pl vb
[X1-5: vb in -t

[N7 & 01-6: sg vb
[X1-5: vb in -ed

fact be opting for a different syntactic interpretation. The sentence can be taken not only as *Pure love and impure love* ... (justifying a plural verb) but also as *Love that is both pure and impure* ... (necessitating a singular).

No such double interpretation is possible with the other sets. The result profile for X1 is somewhat similar to that for N7 and indeed there is a close similarity in the result profiles of all in Category X, which deals with the variant inflections *-ed* and *-t* for the preterite and past participles of *spoil* and *smell*. In the case of *spoil* (X1–2) there is a slight preponderance in favour of the *-t* form for both inflections, though as the wide band of overlap in the '+' column shows there is considerable tolerance for both forms. In the case of *smell* (X3–5) there is equal consistency but the preference for the *-t* forms is rather greater. It is to be noted that the test technique was not sensitive to the distinction between transitive and intransitive use of *smell* nor to the distinction between preterite and past participle that has been detected in 'forced-choice' selection tests (*cf* Quirk 1970a and 1970b), though the difference in score in the '1' column for X1 and X2 is doubtless referable to the fact that the *-ed* ending is more to be preferred for the preterite than for the past participle.

In the sets O1–6, concerned with number concord, there is an interesting fluctuation throughout the acceptability range but close agreement between the results of the three types of test. O2 and O5 show a disagreement that is both interesting and surprising. We have said above that the 'S' and '1' scores should closely correspond, while the '+' score might show some discrepancy. With O2 and O5 the '+' and '1' scores are in harmony with each other and in slight disharmony with the 'S' score. The discrepancy between the results of the judgment and performance tests for O5 is to be explained in relation to the prescriptive teaching on number concord with *none*. The '+' and '1' verdicts are more in line with the school teaching that *none* takes a singular verb than is the performance test. In performance it is likely that our usage is influenced by the structure of the noun phrase in which *none* appears. It is noteworthy that the judgment components for O5 and O6 are in closer agreement than are the selections. *None of the children* caused the selection of a plural verb more frequently than did *Of the thirty critics, none.* We might add that, although the tendency is so small as to be almost negligible, the sets O3 and O4 show a parallel trend in having a discrepancy between selection and judgment, and what discrepancy there is doubtless reflects the same influence of prescriptivism. That is, *each* is used with the plural by more subjects than are prepared to *approve* the use of the plural. And one can even parallel the distinction dependent on the structural place of *each* that we have noted for *none*: *Each of the children* caused the selection of a plural verb more frequently than did *Of twenty reviewers, each*.

The discrepancy between the selection and judgment results for O2 has a somewhat similar explanation. In the selection test the subject *fewer than two students* (an unnatural periphrasis for *one*) was given a plural verb by almost everyone, just as in O1 the logically converse but idiomatic *more than one student* was given a singular verb. On the other hand, while the judgment tests fully endorsed the singular for O1, the unnaturalness of O2 presumably caused subjects to reflect on its logically singular reference and in consequence increased the number opting for the plural. Indeed, it would seem that with Category O subjects are often concerned to treat the judgment tests in terms of what is correct rather than what sounds natural.

5. RATING AND RANKING TESTS

There were three preference tests which had no corresponding selection tests: W1–3. The tests in this category were concerned with alternative forms of the negative of three auxiliaries: *need* (W1), *have* (W2) and *dare* (W3). The relevant results are as follows:

		'+' rating (%)	'I' ranking (%)
W1	*need not*	89	80
	does not need to	77	58
W2	*doesn't have*	76	40
	hasn't	63	30
	hasn't got	84	60
W3	*did not dare ø*	70	45
	dared not	70	50
	did not dare to	69	36

There is a high measure of acceptance for both negative forms of *need*, with greater preference for *need not*. There is more variation in the degree of acceptance of the three forms of *have* (with *a car* as object) but a clearer distinction in the ranking section for preference for *hasn't got*. With the negative forms of *dare*, all three are judged equally acceptable, but the form *did not dare to* emerges as the least preferred in the ranking section.

It should be noted that while Category X tests show a close connection between selection and ranking, Category W rankings are sharply at variance with performance data. From several experiments (*eg* QS 117) the negative of *needs to V, have a car/job/salary* and *dared to V* was given as follows:

needn(o)t	12	(15%)
doesn(o)t need to	68	(85%)
don(o)t have	119	(49%)
haven(o)t	103	(42%)
haven(o)t got	21	(9%)
didn(o)t dare ø	15	(15%)
dared not	17	(17%)
didn(o)t dare to	68	(68%)

The most striking discrepancy is with *need*: in the selection test, *doesn(o)t need to* is selected by 85 per cent of the subjects and *needn(o)t* by a mere 15 per cent, whereas in the ranking test there is a reverse preference: 58 per cent for *does not need to* and 80 per cent for *need not*. But with *dare* and *have* also, the discrepancy is conspicuous. It is not clear why preference and selection should be at variance, but the possibility cannot be ruled out that the selection test can bias results in favour of whatever may be regarded as the regular form – that is, the form representing the most general rule. The general rule for negation of verbs in English requires the auxiliary *do*. This may well account for the fact that the selections gave this form of negation as predominant for all three verbs. But there are other factors, and it is not easy to say which of the two tests, selection or preference, corresponds the more closely to actual usage. In the case of *dare* and *need*, usage is so infrequent that it is difficult to obtain enough corpus data to provide adequate information (but *cf* Svartvik 1968). The same applies, broadly speaking, to *have*, since although this verb occurs commonly enough it is clear that the grammar of negation depends upon the complement involved (in effect, upon the individual meanings of *have*); *cf*

> The medicine had no effect. – *The medicine hadn't got any effect.
> He hasn't (got) a penny. – *He has no penny.
> Snakes do not have legs. – *Snakes have not legs.

These examples raise two further points. While *haven't got* and *haven't* share a meaning which puts them on an equal footing in a preference test, there is no reason to expect them both to be correspondingly elicited in a selection test which seeks the negative of *have*. It is not merely that *haven't got* has in any case its 'own' positive form, *have got*: in the preference test one is offering a number of sentences with a meaning relation between them, while in selection tests one is concerned with more purely grammatical relations. The second point is the appearance in these examples of the negative with *no*. The instructions for performance tests give subjects the option of negation only in the verb phrase. But examination of the Survey of English Usage files shows that negation of *have*-sentences is more frequently recorded in the complement structure (especially *no + N*) than in the verb phrase (even taking all forms of verb phrase negation together).

However, selection and preference results must be considered in relation to the distinction between preference in performance and preference in judgment. What comes to a subject most naturally in the former may not seem preferable when he is confronted by a rarer variant. If we may take a lexical analogy, given the following sentences to complete

[*a*] A man who gives a great deal to charity is ------

[*b*] A man who doesn't easily believe what he's told is ------

subjects who respond with 'kind' and 'suspicious' may not offer the same result if presented with a choice of

[*a*] kind/generous/benevolent

[*b*] suspicious/sceptical/incredulous

Chapter 10

Conclusion

In discussing the experiments described in the present book, we have been concerned with developments in techniques as well as with results of direct linguistic interest. Several new types of test have been introduced and the range now in use is summarised in *Fig* 2. Certain tests require visual presentation and written response; there has been experimentation with oral presentation and oral response; but for the most part the tests have been designed for a mixture of media – oral presentation with written response. In the present study, we have confined our attention to only two types of performance test (compliance and selection), but all the types of judgment tests displayed in *Fig* 2 have been discussed. It seems likely that additional experiments in the immediate future will increasingly exploit visual presentation, which is already being used fruitfully in current forced-choice selection work and which seems inevitable for the investigation of linguistic structures requiring lengthy sentential or multi-sentential context. Visual presentation seems to be equally demanded for stylistic studies, since it is doubtful whether many stylistic parameters can manifest themselves within the limits of the rather brief sentence necessitated by oral presentation.

We have argued in Chapter 4 that responses in compliance tests are not seriously inhibited by an 'explicit' instruction, which in effect tells subjects that they should not rectify sentences that seem to them deviant. On the contrary, the inclusion of such an explicit instruction makes it easier to evaluate results, since we need not fear that subjects have interpreted the requirement of the tests variously. Just as not all subjects needed the explicit instruction, so not all of them appeared to need practice. But rather detailed scrutiny of the position revealed that subjects' responses

after the first ten sentences seemed somewhat more reliable than those
for the first ten. Indeed, it transpired that there was an interdependence
between explicit instruction and practice, and that the optimum results
were obtained when subjects were given both the explicit instruction and
a practice set of ten sentences. Such practice has been investigated only
with compliance tests, but it is reasonable to extend the recommendation
for practice to other types of test.

Even more important as a guarantee that the responses in all tests are
comparable is the presentation of the test items in more than one sequence.
There are two relevant variables: the absolute position in a battery
(especially whether an item is near the beginning or end) and the position
of an item relative to other items in the battery (since responses may be
influenced by the immediately preceding item or by the fact that other
items of the same test category have or have not already been presented).
In consequence, on the basis of our experiments reported in Chapter 4,
we have recommended that each battery should be given in two sequences,
the second being a total reversal (*eg* 50–1) of the first, since this takes
account of both the relevant variables. It would be advisable for each order
to be tested with a similar number of subjects.

The preceding point presupposes that each battery is presented to
more than one group of subjects. Since our aim is to produce a set of
responses as representative as possible of the total linguistic population in
which we are interested, we have regarded it as important that each
battery in each presentation order be tested with more than one group, so
that we can form an opinion on the degree to which any one group is
representative. We have concluded in Chapter 5 that several groups of
subjects need to be tested with each battery if the sum of responses is to
be satisfactorily complementary (*cf Fig* 5).

By 'group' we understand a body of subjects taking the battery at the
same time and in the same room, and hence under the same conditions.
'Same conditions' includes importantly the same acoustic conditions,
and care must be taken to ensure that the room used allows a tape-recording to be heard with equal clarity by all members of the group. Moreover,
it is not merely physical conditions that constitute a serious variable. As
we have shown in Chapter 6, results can reflect the opinion that subjects
form on the purpose of the experiment. To ensure, therefore, the maximum comparability of results, groups taking the same battery should do
so under conditions which as nearly as possible suggest identity of purpose. Since, however, it is impossible to achieve absolute parity, it is
important to elicit each subject's opinion as to the experiment's purpose,

so that it becomes at least theoretically possible to make allowance for a variable which is especially intractable.

This is tantamount to saying that as well as being concerned with the extent to which a group of subjects constitutes an appropriate sample of the total population, we are concerned that a subject's responses should be an appropriate sample of his own linguistic use and attitude. To this end, we have conducted experiments to see how consistent a subject is with himself – in general, with reassuring results (Chapter 5). We have also found that a subject's responses in compliance tests are consistent even when evaluation tests intervene. It would therefore seem that we need not rule out the use of the same subjects for more than one battery.

The subjects' responses are themselves of widely differing types, but for the most part they are directly usable as data for the linguist. This is above all true for the judgment tests, where evaluation, similarity, rating, and ranking responses are ready-made data. For the performance results, this is scarcely less true so far as the selection tests are concerned. With the compliance tests, however, the relationship between the subject's response and the linguistic datum is indirect and sophisticated. The essential factor in the relationship is the concept of the 'RNC' (*Fig* 4 and *p* 20), the criteria for which are determined by the linguist and derived from the specific aim which he has set for the test and which reflect his hypothesis as to where the linguistic problem lies and what constitutes an 'evasion' of it. While responses other than RNCs – even the slightest sign of hesitation – are of relevance as an index of the subject's reaction to the test problem, the RNCs are overwhelmingly the most important and in point of fact in the present study we have used them almost exclusively. We intend, however, in a separate publication, to show the way in which RNCs co-occur with other types of non-compliance and with hesitations and the relationship of this co-occurrence to test category. In addition, we are investigating the doubtless more direct relation between (for example) form selected by a subject in performance test and form approved by him in judgment test.

Correlations undertaken already and reported in Chapter 9 have been based not on a comparison of the individual's responses but on the total responses of all subjects. The results are of considerable interest. While *Figs* 14a and 14b show that there can be a general close agreement between an RNC response in performance and a rejection (minus) response in judgment throughout the entire score range, the discussion of *Figs* 14c and 14d draws attention to interesting generalisations about the test types which yield sharply different results in performance and judgment. Thus, the rejection score is considerably higher where the deviance is predominantly semantic, and the RNC score is considerably higher where the test problem predominantly concerns positional deviance. So too in considering the results of the similarity test with those of the evaluation test (*Fig* 15), we have found that the correlation brings together in a significant way sentences with repeated adverb which are objectionable stylistically (*eg* A6, A8, A9), and contrasts them with repeated adverb sentences which are tautologous without the stylistic objection (*eg* B1, B2, B5).

Of course, we must not forget that responses elicited in a test situation can never be generalised in a simple way so as to be equated with actual use and attitude. On the other hand, it is clear that our results have repeatedly endorsed the distinctions postulated in *Fig* 1. Thus, the distinction between potential and habitual use and the distinction between a tolerant attitude and an attitude governed by precept are well illustrated in comparing the selection, compliance, and preference results for the category O tests discussed on *pp* 76 *f*. Again, there is the striking contrast between potential behaviour and attitude as exemplified in the sharply different compliance and evaluation results for tests Q1 and Q2: *cf pp* 100 *f*.

Our principal source of acceptability data has remained the compliance test, with the RNC in turn as the principal index. But while RNCs are crucial in the interpretation of the responses, it is important to recognise that they are not an absolute measure of deviance, but are relative only to a specific type as represented in our test batteries by the 'category'. Thus the number of RNCs can very valuably measure the relative unacceptability of tests within the same category (*eg* U1 and U2), but comparison of scores in different categories would be very misleading (*eg* U1 and T1). Not only, as we have explained, are the criteria for RNCs thoroughly category-specific: there is a second reason why RNC totals are relative. There are some types of deviance that appear to evoke RNCs more readily than others. For example, in Battery IV the sentence 'Every the man day her visited' (universally rejected in the evaluation test) caused only 25 per cent of subjects to make RNCs, whereas the less grossly unacceptable sentence 'They have done it last week' caused 60 per cent of the subjects to make RNCs. It is important to realise [a] that performance of the task in each case required subjects in some sense to perceive the structure of the test sentences correctly; [b] that rectification was in principle no easier in the latter case than in the former; and [c] that all subjects had been given the instruction not to carry out any rectification. It would seem to follow therefore that the RNCs (all, in fact, rectifications) were carried out unconsciously in the latter case. In other words, the deviance of the former instance may be presumed to be so conspicuous that subjects could treat it as deliberately so and thus find it the easier to obey the explicit instruction to carry out the task and nothing else.

Moreover, even within the same test category RNC totals may be incommensurable if different tasks are involved. Of course, as we have already stated in the concluding paragraph of Chapter 8, a given test sentence will in general produce a similar number of RNCs with one operation task as with another, but we pointed out two important exceptions to this situation. The first is where one task, but not another, sharply alters relations within the test sentence. The second is where one task rather than another appears to oblige subjects to analyse the sentence more radically; in the subsequent re-synthesis it is natural that subjects put it into a form that better accords with the general rules of the language.

For we must emphasise that the instances of deviance incorporated in test batteries are not anecdotal instances of isolated peculiarities but are selected as canonically representing major principles of sentence formation and specific aspects of use and attitude.

Our experience has nevertheless shown how difficult it is to specify the grammatical and lexical territory delimited by a canonical form. Thus, a class of items may be acceptable in certain positions in one form of a sentence but become unacceptable in some of those positions in another form of the sentence. The class exemplified by *today* may occupy initial position in the declarative form but not in the interrogative; *cf* H15:

Today, the museum was open.
The museum was open today.
Was the museum open today?
*Today, was the museum open?

Similarly, while *badly* collocates lexically with the verb *need* irrespective of clause-transformation (*cf* Greenbaum 1970), our tests (D1 in III and IIIa) have shown that the position of *badly* is relatively restricted in interrogative clauses:

He needed the money badly.
Did he need the money badly?
He badly needed the money.
?Did he badly need the money?
5

On the other hand, a class of items may be acceptable in one form of a sentence but not in another, irrespective of position; *cf* H6:

> Surprisingly, it's in the papers.
> *Surprisingly, is it in the papers?
> It's in the papers, surprisingly.
> *Is it in the papers, surprisingly?

Thus in the case of H15, if *today* is in initial position there is easy and obvious rectification by transposition, whilst in H6 subjects are generally forced either to omit *surprisingly* or to replace it by a paraphrase. It may be further noted that

> Somehow the message had got through.
> Somehow the message hadn't got through.

contrast not only in being affirmative and negative but in having a difference in meaning as between 'in some way' and 'for some reason'. In the affirmative sentence, *somehow* is a manner adverbial, and the position is that even where manner adverbials can operate initially in affirmative sentences, they cannot do so in negative sentences, as our experiments have shown conclusively.

This last example illustrates the way in which semantic considerations become predominant in the explication of syntactic deviance. It seems clear that if elicitation procedures are to provide 'the operational connexion between the linguist's "raw material" and its ultimate source of control in the reactions of native speakers' (Lyons 1968, 138), much fundamental work must be done on the relations between syntax and semantics. Useful references to exploratory experimental work in semantics are given in Leech 1969, 266. Meanwhile, our test batteries are producing data which both are directly assimilable into the description of English (as in Greenbaum 1969a) and offer the linguistic theorist material for evaluating such concepts as 'deep' and 'surface', 'competence' and 'performance'.

Tabular appendices

KEY 1 *Battery*: The composition of groups taking particular batteries is
given on *pp* 37 *f*.

2 *Seq(uence) no* refers to the position of the test in the battery as
presented to subjects; this information is given for Battery I in
Tables 1, 8 and 11; for Batteries II and III (where sequence differed with different groups) in Tables 17–23; Battery IIIa has the
same sequence as Battery III Order (i), Table 18; Battery IV tests
were presented in the order shown in Tables 15 and 16.

3 *Cat(egory) no* refers to the designation of the test based on a categorisation of the linguistic problems investigated. The nature of
the categories is explained in Chapter 7.

4 *Task*: T and S under this head mean 'task announced before sentence' and 'sentence announced before task' respectively. Tasks
that are abbreviated as for example 'N^1: *child*' indicate that the
first noun is to be replaced by *child*.

5 *RNC* indicates the responses scored as Relevant Non-Compliance
(*p* 20). The criteria for scoring are explained in Chapter 7 for
Batteries I-IIIa and on *pp* 52 *f* for Battery IV.

6 The test sentences are given in a prosodic transcription explained
in Crystal and Quirk 1964.

Table 1

Compliance tests : Battery I

Seq no	Cat no	TEST SENTENCE	Task	RNC n=85	scores %
8	A1	in/dĕed# /some people indèed attempted it#	T/present	26	31
11	A2	/rĕally# the /students réally wòrk during the term#	T/N¹: student	8	9
13	A3	/cĕrtainly# your /children cértainly dislìked me#	S/N¹: child	11	13
17	A4	/hŏnestly# Mr /Jones honestly believed our stòry#	S/present	12	14
33	A5	/neverthelĕss# /some people neverthelèss attempted it#	S/present	12	14
36	A6	/ŏnly# the /students ónly wòrk during the term#	T/N¹: student	6	7
38	A7	/ălso# your /children álso dislìked me#	S/N¹: child	7	8
42	A8	/hŏnestly# /Mr Jones honestly reported our stòry#	S/present	6	7
4	B1	in/dĕed# /many soldiers thòroughly hated it#	T/present	8	9
19	B2	/rĕally# your /children ábsolutely hòwl every night#	T/N¹: child	2	2
22	B3	/cĕrtainly# his /workers entírely distrùsted him#	S/N¹: worker	11	13
24	B4	/hŏnestly# /Mrs Smith totally rejected his gìft#	T/present	11	13
29	B5	/frănkly# they were /really appalled by their lèader#	S/N¹: he	12	14
44	B6	/frănkly# the /workers were honestly answered by the mànager#	T/N¹: worker	7	8
47	B7	/hăppily# /most of them fortunately admired the achìevement#	T/present	9	11
49	B8	/pĕrsonally# /I mysĕlf# ap/pròved of the idea#	S/present	9	11
1	C1	his /sons completely managed the family bùsiness#	S/present	3	4
26	C2	his /sons managed the family business complètely#	S/present	15	18

Seq no	Cat no	TEST SENTENCE	Task	RNC scores $n=85$	%
3	C4	my /friend entirely prepares the mèals#	T/past	7	8
28	C5	my /friend prepares the meals entìrely#	T/past	17	20
18	C7	/our men fully observe Jòhn#	S/past	12	14
43	C8	/our men observe John fùlly#	T/past	13	15
20	C10	the /students utterly expected his arrìval#	T/present	7	8
45	C11	the /students expected his arrival ùtterly#	S/present	39	46
6	E1	the /council slightly lowered his rènt#	S/present	6	7
31	E2	the /council lowered his rènt slightly#	T/present	10	12
10	E3	the /girl faintly fròwned#	S/present	33	39
35	E4	the /girl fròwned faintly#	T/present	11	13
12	E5	I /differ profòundly from him#	T/negative	21	25
37	E6	I /differ from him profòundly#	S/negative	26	31
15	E7	she com/pletely agrèed#	T/negative	22	26
40	E8	she a/greed complètely#	T/negative	30	35
16	E9	he /virtually is ruling the còuntry#	T/N[1]: *they*	65	76
41	E10	he is /virtually ruling the còuntry#	S/N[1]: *they*	5	6
21	E11	the /price practically has dòubled#	S/N[1]: *prices*	67	79
46	E12	the /price has practically dòubled#	S/N[1]: *prices*	2	2
25	E13	he /hardly could sit stìll#	S/N[1]: *they*	54	63
50	E14	he could /hardly sit stìll#	S/N[1]: *they*	1	1
2	F1	he will /possibly become a tèacher#	S/negative	61	72
27	F2	he can /probably drive a càr#	T/negative	81	95
9	F3	he can /certainly drive a càr#	S/negative	85	100
34	F4	he can /usually write wèll#	S/negative	33	39
30	H1	how/ěver# he /started a new bùsiness#	S/question	64	75
5	H4	confi/děntially# he is a /fòol#	S/question	9	11

Table 1 (*continued*)

Seq no	Cat no	TEST SENTENCE	Task	RNC scores n = 85	%
7	H5	/străngely# they re/fuse to pày#	T/question	61 (i)	72
51				65 (ii)	76
39	H7	/cĕrtainly# the /car broke dòwn#	T/question	65	76
14	H9	/ăctually# she /sat nèar him#	S/question	71	83
32	H14	/mŭsically# the /concert was a succèss#	T/question	66	78
23	H15	to/dăy# the mu/seum was òpen#	T/question	79	93
48	H16	/sŭddenly# he /opened the dòor#	T/question	82	96

Table 2

Compliance tests : Battery II

Cat no	TEST SENTENCE	Task	RNC scores n = 179	%
A1	in/dĕed# /some people indèed attempted it#	T/present	32	18
A9	/ăctually# /some lectures are actually given before tèn#	T/past	29	16
A10	/sŭrely# the /child surely apologises for his mistàkes#	S/past	46	26
A11	/thĕrefore# /many seats are therefore booked a week befòre#	T/past	52	29
A12	/sŭddenly# the /woman suddenly a:grees to the plàn#	S/past	70	39
A13	/pĕrsonally# /I pĕrsonally# ap/pròved of the idea#	S/present	30	17
A14	/lŭckily# your /father luckily owns a càr#	T/past	43	24
B9	/rĕally# your /children often hòwl during the night#	S/N[1]: *child*	13	7
B10	/many soldiers thòroughly hated it#	T/present	9	5
B11	/hŏnestly# /Mrs Smith rejected his gìft#	S/present	10	6

Cat no	TEST SENTENCE	Task	RNC scores n = 179	%
C3	the /family business was completely managed by his sòns#	S/present	11	6
C6	the /meals are entirely prepared by my frìend#	S/past	10	6
C9	/John is fully observed by our mèn#	T/past	9	5
C12	his ar/rival was utterly expected by the stùdents#	S/present	40	22
F5	she has /wisely refused your òffer#	T/negative	148	83
F6	he has /kindly accepted our invitàtion#	S/negative	137	77
F7	I can /fortunately understand her mèssage#	T/negative	157 (i) 106 (ii)	88 59
F8	he can /often explain what they mèan#	T/negative	36	20
F9	I can /really believe what they sày#	T/negative	36	20
H2	inci/dĕntally# /he is the chàirman#	S/question	49	27
H6	/it's in the pàpers [sur/prìsingly#]#	T/question	110	61
H10	he /rightly decided to make a wìll#	S/question	66	37
H11	he will /probably stay làte#	S/question	49	27
H12	they will /possibly leave èarly#	T/question	45	25
H13	they will per/haps come sòon#	T/question	31	17
J1	ex/cept Sŭnday# he /works every dày#	S/past	29	16
J3	ex/cept for Sŭnday# he /works every dày#	S/past	16	9
K1	they are /leaving the country due to ill-hèalth#	S/N¹: he	23	13
K2	they are /selling the house because of the gàrden#	T/N¹: he	2	1
L1	he must /put the tráy# be/tween you and Ì#	S/negative	34	19
L2	she's /very clèver# be/tween you and Í#	S/negative	22	12
M1	/judging from your remărks# /nobody spèaks to him#	S/past	17	9

Table 2 (*continued*)

Cat no	TEST SENTENCE	Task	RNC scores n=179	%
M2	/walking through the cóllege# i/deas còme to him#	T/past	48	27
M3	/living in Lóndon# /finding work is no pròblem#	S/past	34	19
M4	/sèriously spéaking# /making friends is no pròblem#	S/past	13	7
P2	I /think he's not stàying#	T/N¹: *she*	5	3
P4	he /doesn't know she's còming#	S/N¹: *I*	2	1
Q1	/John broke the wìndow# /but he refused to pày for it#	T/question	160	89
Q2	/she washed the cúp# /but he refused to drìnk from it#	S/question	177	99
R1	he /hated the men's working làte#	S/question	55	31
R3	she /hated their coming èarly#	S/question	32	18

Table 3

Compliance tests : Battery III

Cat no	TEST SENTENCE	Task	RNC scores n=117	%
A15	/lŭckily# the /game luckily ends at sèven#	S/past	57	44
A16	sur/prĭsingly# your /father surprisingly owns a càr#	T/past	22	19
B12	in/dĕed# /many soldiers hàted it#	T/present	1	1
B13	/Mrs Smith totally rejected his gìft#	T/present	6	5
D1	he /badly needed the mòney#	T/question	65	56
D2	they /badly wounded the èlephant#	S/question	69	59
D3	they /badly treated the sèrvant#	S/question	89	76
D4	she /deeply admired the spèech#	S/question	34	29
D5	they /deeply drilled the hòle#	S/question	89	76
D6	he /deeply slept that nìght#	S/question	100	86
F10	you could /always send it this afternŏon#	S/negative	81	69

Cat no	TEST SENTENCE	Task	RNC scores n = 117	%
F11	they could /always go there tomòrrow#	T/negative	70	60
F12	you should /always take it before dìnner#	S/negative	70	60
G1	under/stăndably# they /opened the lètter#	S/negative	7	6
G2	/sŭddenly# the /man wouldn't move the car any fùrther#	T/N[1]: *he*	0	0
G3	/sŭddenly# he /drove the car further ahèad#	S/negative	48	41
G4	re/lŭctantly# they in/sisted on his resignàtion#	S/negative	27	23
H8	the /car certainly broke dòwn#	S/question	63	54
H11	he will /probably stay làte#	T/question	27	23
I1	she has /spoken to him yèt#	T/question	2	2
I2	she has /mentioned it at àll#	T/question	2	2
L3	be/tween you and Ĭ# she's /very clèver#	S/negative	7	6
S1	she en/joys novels whose heroes survìve#	T/N[1]: *they*	4	3
T1	the /house is perfectly good enough for thèm#	T/N[1]: *houses*	0	0
U1	/David is the one who I think comes règularly#	S/N[1]: *he*	9	8
U2	/Nòrman is the one who plays I think fréquently#	S/N[1]: *he*	75	64
V1	the /man has a better job than was thòught#	T/N[1]: *he*	2	2
V2	the /man has a smaller salary than was thòught he had#	S/N[1]: *he*	50	43
Y1	/Alice is both older but happier than she wàs#	S/N[1]: *she*	98	84
Z1	his /wife is a càt# but /hĕ# I /lìke#	S/N[1]: *she*	36	31

6

Table 4

Compliance tests : Battery IIIa

Cat no	TEST SENTENCE	Task	RNC scores n=70	%
A15	/lŭckily# the /game luckily ends at sèven#	S/past	43	61
A16	sur/prĭsingly# your /father surprisingly owns a càr#	T/N[1]: parents	23	33
B12	in/dĕed# /many soldiers hàted it#	T/negative	3	4
B13	/Mrs Smith totally rejected his gìft#	T/question	0	0
D1	he /badly needed the mòney#	T/N[1]: they	0	0
D2	they /badly wounded the èlephant#	S/present	15	21
D3	they /badly treated the sèrvant#	S/present	46	66
D4	she /deeply admired the spèech#	S/present	6	9
D5	they /deeply drilled the hòle#	S/present	38	54
D6	he /deeply slept all nìght#	S/present	47	67
F10	you could /always send it this afternŏon#	S/negative	55	79
F11	they /couldn't always go there tomòrrow#	T/Adv[3]: this afternoon	7	10
F12	you /shouldn't always take it before dìnner#	S/N[3]: lunch	1	1
G1	under/stăndably# they /didn't open the lètter#	S/present	6	9
G2	/sŭddenly# the /man wouldn't move the car any fùrther#	T/N[1]: men	1	1
G3	/sŭddenly# he /doesn't drive the car further ahèad#	S/past	1	1
G4	re/lŭctantly# they /don't insist on his resignàtion#	S/past	9	13
H8	the /car certainly broke dòwn#	S/question	31	44
H11	/will he probably stay láte#	T/Adv[2]: till Monday	4	6
I1	she has /spoken to him yèt#	T/question	1	1
I2	she has /mentioned it at àll#	T/negative	2	3
L3	be/tween you and Ĭ# she's /very clèver#	S/question	23	33
N3	/Mr Jones and therefore his sŏn# is re/signing from the pàrty#	T/question	14	20

Cat no	TEST SENTENCE	Task	RNC scores n = 70	%
N4	/John as well as occasionally Hǎrry# /visit the schòol#	T/question	64	91
N6	/Mr Brown in addition to his wǐfe# /stay for lùnch#	S/question	67	96
N7	/pure and impure love attracts the nòvelists#	T/question	31	44
O2	/fewer than two students passes the exàm#	T/question	64	91
O3	/each of the children win a prìze#	T/question	41	59
O4	of /twenty revíewers# /each like my bòok#	S/Num: *ten*	45	64
O5	/none of the children answer the quèstion#	T/question	49	70
O6	of /thirty crítics# /none like your shòw#	S/Num: *ten*	26	37
S1	she en/joys novels whose heroes survìve#	T/V[1]: past	2	3
T1	the /house is perfectly good enough for thèm#	T/past	1	1
U1	/David is the one who I think comes règularly#	S/N[1]: *he*	11	16
U2	/Nòrman is the one who plays I think fréquently#	S/3xV: past	57	81
V1	the /man has a better job than was thòught#	T/negative	18	26
V2	the /man has a smaller salary than was thòught he had#	S/V[1]: negative	32	46
X1	they have /spoilt my hòliday#	T/negative	1	1
X2	his /mother spòilt him always#	S/Adv: *never*	0	0
X3	/I smelt ònions cooking sómewhere#	T/N[1]: *we*	3	4
X4	the /dinner smelt àwful again last níght#	T/N[1]: *it*	0	0
X5	I have /smelt the flòwers#	T/negative	1	1
Y1	/Alice is both older but happier than she wàs#	S/N[1]: *the girls*	52	74
Z1	his /wife is a càt# but /hě# I /lìke#	S/N[1]: *she*	25	36

Table 5

Selection tests : Battery II

Cat no	TEST SENTENCE	Task		Selected form n = 179	%
N1	/Mary and Wïlliam# /sometimes came to tèa#	S/present	sg pl	0 141	0 100
N2	/John and sometimes Hărry# /visited the schòol#	T/present	sg pl	20 113	15 85
P1	I /think he's còming#	S/negative	V1 V2	146 18	89 11
P3	I /know they're stàying#	T/negative	V1 V2	108 60	64 36

Table 6

Selection tests : Battery III

Cat no	TEST SENTENCE	Task		Selected form n = 117	%
N3	/Mr Jones and therefore his sŏn# re/signed from the pàrty#	T/present	sg pl	32 77	29 71
N4	/John as well as occasionally Hărry# /visited the schòol#	T/present	sg pl	66 12	85 15
N5	/Mr Smith with his sŏn# /left for Lòndon#	T/present	sg pl	93 16	85 15
N6	/Mr Brown in addition to his wïfe# /stayed for lùnch#	S/present	sg pl	88 22	80 20
N7	/pure and impure love attracted the nòvelists#	T/present	sg pl	45 69	40 60
O1	/more than one student attended the lèctures#	T/present	sg pl	104 12	90 10
O2	/fewer than two students passed the exàm#	T/present	sg pl	7 104	6 94
O3	/each of the children won a prìze#	T/present	sg pl	100 15	87 13
O4	of /twenty revíewers# /each praised my bòok#	S/present	sg pl	103 10	91 9
O5	/none of the children answered the quèstion#	T/present	sg pl	64 51	56 44
O6	of /thirty crítics# /none praised your shòw#	S/present	sg pl	73 40	65 35

Cat no	TEST SENTENCE	Task	Selected form n = 117		%
X1	they have /ruined my hòliday#	T/V: *spoil*	-*ed*	53	46
			-*t*	62	54
X2	his /mother spòils him always#	S/past	-*ed*	52	47
			-*t*	59	53
X3	/I smell càbbage cooking sómewhere#	T/past	-*ed*	37	32
			-*t*	78	68
X4	the /dinner smells àwful again toníght#	T/past	-*ed*	41	37
			-*t*	69	63
X5	I have ar/ranged the flòwers#	T/V: *smell*	-*ed*	46	40
			-*t*	69	60

Table 7

Selection tests : Battery IIIa

Cat no	TEST SENTENCE	Task	Selected form n = 70		%
N5	/Mr Smith with his sŏn# /left for Lòndon#	T/present	sg	11	17
			pl	54	83
O1	/more than one student attended the lèctures#	T/present	sg	62	90
			pl	7	10

Table 8

Evaluation tests : Battery I

Seq no	Cat no	TEST SENTENCE	n = 85 +	?	−	% 'minus'
8	A1	in/dĕed# /some people indèed attempted it#	8	17	60	71
11	A2	/rĕally# the /students réally wòrk during the term#	24	23	38	45
13	A3	/cĕrtainly# your /children cértainly dislìked me#	15	28	42	49
17	A4	/hŏnestly# /Mr Jones honestly believed our stòry#	22	24	39	46
33	A5	/neverthelĕss# /some people neverthelèss attempted it#	11	21	53	62
36	A6	/ŏnly# the /students ónly wòrk during the term#	9	18	58	68

Table 8 (*continued*)

Seq no	Cat no	TEST SENTENCE	$+$	?	$-$	% 'minus'
				n = 85		
38	A7	/ălso# /your children álso disliked me#	19	20	46	54
42	A8	/hŏnestly# /Mr Jones honestly reported our stòry#	29	17	39	46
4	B1	in/dĕed# /many soldiers thòroughly hated it#	75	4	6	7
19	B2	/rĕally# your /children ábsolutely hòwl every night#	58	11	16	19
22	B3	/cĕrtainly# /his workers entírely distrùsted him#	55	14	16	19
24	B4	/hŏnestly# /Mrs Smith totally rejected his gìft#	59	16	10	12
29	B5	/frănkly# they were /really appalled by their lèader#	71	11	3	4
44	B6	/frănkly# the /workers were honestly answered by the mànager#	51	11	23	27
47	B7	/hăppily# /most of them fortunately admired the achìevement#	11	17	57	67
49	B8	/pĕrsonally# /I mysĕlf# ap/pròved of the idea#	44	10	31	36
1	C1	his /sons completely managed the family bùsiness#	62	13	10	12
26	C2	his /sons managed the family business complètely#	67	6	12	14
3	C4	my /friend entirely prepares the mèals#	48	18	19	22
28	C5	my /friend prepares the meals entìrely#	69	10	6	7
18	C7	/our men fully observe Jòhn#	50	17	18	21
43	C8	/our men observe John fùlly#	68	10	7	8
20	C10	the /students utterly expected his arrìval#	26	21	38	45
45	C11	the /students expected his arrival ùtterly#	6	13	66	78
6	E1	the /council slightly lowered his rènt#	63	9	13	15
31	E2	the /council lowered his rènt slightly#	82	0	3	4

Seq no	Cat no	TEST SENTENCE	n=85 +	?	−	% 'minus'
10	E3	the /girl faintly fròwned#	44	23	18	21
35	E4	the /girl fròwned faintly#	79	2	4	5
12	E5	I /differ profòundly from him#	68	12	5	6
37	E6	I /differ from him profòundly#	79	2	4	5
15	E7	she com/pletely agrèed#	77	5	3	4
40	E8	she a/greed complètely#	83	1	1	1
16	E9	he /virtually is ruling the còuntry#	19	27	39	46
41	E10	he is /virtually ruling the còuntry#	84	1	0	0
21	E11	the /price practically has dòubled#	13	24	48	56
46	E12	the /price has practically dòubled#	84	0	1	1
25	E13	he /hardly could sit stìll#	16	23	46	54
50	E14	he could /hardly sit stìll#	85	0	0	0
2	F1	he /won't possibly become a tèacher#	12	13	60	71
27	F2	he /can't probably drive a càr#	3	3	79	93
9	F3	he /can't certainly drive a càr#	3	7	75	88
34	F4	he /can't usually write wèll#	46	15	24	28
30	H1	how/ĕver# /did he start a new búsiness#	37	23	25	29
5	H4	confi/dĕntially# /is he a fóol#	71	10	4	5
7	H5	/străngely# /do they refuse to páy#	6	14	65 (i)	76
51			3	12	70 (ii)	82
39	H7	/cĕrtainly# /did the car break dówn#	1	12	72	85
14	H9	/ăctually# /did she sit néar him#	40	20	25	29
32	H14	/mŭsically# /was the concert a succéss#	57	11	17	20
23	H15	to/dăy# /was the museum ópen#	16	18	51	60
48	H16	/sŭddenly# /did he open the dóor#	2	7	76	89

Table 9

Evaluation tests: Battery II

Cat no	TEST SENTENCE	n = 179 +	?	−	% 'minus'
A1	in/dĕed# /some people indèed attempted it#	15	48	126	70
A9	/ăctually# /some lectures are actually given before tèn#	30	40	109	61
A10	/sŭrely# the /child surely apologises for his mistàkes#	11	23	145	81
A11	/thĕrefore# /many seats are therefore booked a week befòre#	12	40	127	71
A12	/sŭddenly# the /woman suddenly agrees to the plàn#	13	29	137	77
A13	/pĕrsonally# /I pĕrsonally# ap/pròved of the idea#	15	33	131	73
A14	/lŭckily# your /father luckily owns a càr#	10	29	140	78
B9	/rĕally# your /children often hòwl during the night#	131	31	17	9
B10	/many soldiers thòroughly hated it#	157	15	7	4
B11	/hŏnestly# /Mrs Smith rejected his gìft#	126	30	23	13
C3	the /family business was completely managed by his sòns#	166	7	6	3
C6	the /meals are entirely prepared by my frìend#	158	14	7	4
C9	/John is fully observed by our mèn#	162	14	3	2
C12	his ar/rival was utterly expected by the stùdents#	53	57	69	39
F5	she /hasn't wisely refused your òffer#	31	47	101	56
F6	he /hasn't kindly accepted our invitàtion#	18	41	120	67
F7	I /can't fortunately understand her mèssage#	24 / 48	59 / 45	96 (i) / 86 (ii)	54 / 48
F8	he /can't often explain what they mèan#	162	12	5	3
F9	I /can't really believe what they sày#	176	2	1	1

Cat no	TEST SENTENCE	n = 179 +	?	−	% 'minus'
H2	inci/dĕntally# /is he the cháirman#	167	8	4	2
H3	/is he the cháirman [inci/déntally#]#	136	20	23	13
H6	/is it in the pápers [sur/prísingly#]#	10	37	132	74
H10	/did he rightly decide to make a wíll#	108	44	27	15
H11	/will he probably stay láte#	108	44	27	15
H12	/will they possibly leave éarly#	120	41	18	10
H13	/will they perhaps come sóon#	123	32	24	13
J1	ex/cept Sŭnday# he /worked every dày#	132	28	19	11
J2	he /worked every dăy# ex/cept Sùnday#	158	9	12	7
J3	ex/cept for Sŭnday# he /worked every dày#	159	10	10	6
J4	she /cleaned every dăy# ex/cept for Sùnday#	132	21	26	15
K1	he is /leaving the country due to ill-hèalth#	121	18	40	22
K2	he is /selling the house because of the gàrden#	151	17	11	6
L1	he /mustn't put the trày# be/tween you and Ì#	77	21	81	45
L2	she /isn't very clèver# be/tween you and Í#	54	45	80	45
M1	/judging from your remărks# /nobody spòke to him#	165	9	5	3
M2	/walking through the cóllege# i/deas càme to him#	107	27	45	25
M3	/living in Lóndon# /finding work was no pròblem#	143	17	19	11
M4	/sèriously spéaking# /making friends was no pròblem#	152	16	11	6
N1	/Mary and William# /sometimes comes to tèa#	8	5	166	93
N2	/John and sometimes Hărry# /visits the schòol#	68	28	83	46
P1	I /don't think he's còming#	175	0	4	2
P2	she /thinks he's not stàying#	171	6	2	1
P3	I /know they aren't stàying#	173	4	2	1
P4	I /don't know she's còming#	78	40	61	34

Table 9 (*continued*)

Cat no	TEST SENTENCE	n = 179			% 'minus'
		+	?	−	
Q1	/ did John break the wíndow# /but refuse to páy for it#	132	27	20	11
Q2	/did she wash the cúp# but /he refuse to drínk from it#	81	47	51	28
R1	/did he hate the men's working láte#	108	26	45	25
R2	/did he hate the men working láte#	145	14	20	11
R3	/did she hate their coming éarly#	163	12	4	2
R4	/did she hate them coming éarly#	147	10	22	12

Table 10

Evaluation tests : Battery III

Cat no	TEST SENTENCE	n = 117			% 'minus'
		+	?	−	
A15	/lŭckily# the /game luckily ended at sèven#	8	17	92	79
A16	sur/prĭsingly# your /father surprisingly owns a càr#	3	16	98	84
B12	in/dĕed# /many soldiers hàte it#	110	5	2	2
B13	/Mrs Smith totally rejects his gìft#	106	10	1	1
D1	/did he badly need the móney#	58	34	25	21
D2	/did they badly wound the sóldier#	48	35	34	29
D3	/did they badly treat the sérvant#	16	48	53	45
D4	/did she deeply admire the spéech#	52	41	24	21
D5	/did they deeply drill the hóle#	6	41	70	60
D6	/did he deeply sleep that níght#	4	35	78	67
F10	you /couldn't always send it this afternŏon#	7	22	88	75
F12	you /shouldn't always take it before dìnner#	70	26	21	18
G1	under/stăndably# they /didn't open the lètter#	110	5	2	2
G2	/sŭddenly# he /wouldn't move the car any fùrther#	73	18	26	22
G3	/sŭddenly# he /didn't drive the car further ahèad#	21	21	75	64
G4	re/lŭctantly# they /didn't insist on his resignàtion#	39	33	45	37

Cat no	TEST SENTENCE	n=117 +	?	−	% 'minus'
H8	/did the car certainly break dówn#	31	34	52	44
H11	/will he probably stay láte#	57	36	24	21
L3	be/tween you and Ǐ# she /isn't very clèver#	56	19	42	36
N3	/Mr Jones and therefore his sǒn# re/signs from the pàrty#	33	31	53	45
N4	/John as well as occasionally Hǎrry# /visits the schòol#	48	42	27	23
N5	/Mr Smith with his sǒn# /leaves for Lòndon#	66	29	22	19
N6	/Mr Brown in addition to his wǐfe# /stays for lùnch#	42	44	31	27
S1	they en/joy novels whose heroes survìve#	93	13	11	9
T1	the /houses are perfectly good enough for thèm#	107	7	3	3
T2	the /novels are quite good enough for hìm#	112	2	3	3
U1	/he is the one who I think comes règularly#	89	20	8	7
U2	/hè is the one who plays I think fréquently#	33	52	32	27
V1	/he has a better job than was thòught#	104	10	3	3
V2	he has a /smaller salary than was thòught he had#	49	37	31	26
Y1	she is both /older but happier than she wàs#	50	26	41	35
Z1	/she is a càt# but /hě# I /lìke#	38	23	56	48

Table 11

Similarity tests: Battery I

Seq no	Cat no	TEST SENTENCE	n=64 =	?	≠	% 'equals'
53	A1	in/děed# /some people attèmpted it# /some people indèed attempted it#	30	17	17	47
59	A2	/rěally# the /students wòrk during the term# the /students réally wòrk during the term#	12	5	47	19

Table 11 *(continued)*

Seq no	Cat no	TEST SENTENCE	=	?	≠	% 'equals'
61	A3	your /children cértainly dislìked me# /cĕrtainly# your /children dislìked me#	26	19	19	41
55	A4	/Mr Jones honestly believed our stòry# /hŏnestly# /Mr Jones believed our stòry#	8	10	46	13
66	A5	/nevertheless# /some people attèmpted it# /some people nevertheless attempted it#	53	4	7	83
56	A6	/ŏnly# the /students wòrk during the term# the /students ónly wòrk during the term#	1	1	62	1
68	A7	/ălso# your /children dislìked me# your /children álso dislìked me#	22	15	27	34
63	A8	/hŏnestly# /Mr Jones reported our stòry# /Mr Jones honestly reported our stòry#	3	4	57	5
62	B1	in/dĕed# /many soldiers hàted it# /many soldiers thòroughly hated it#	33	8	23	52
57	B2	your /children ábsolutely hòwl every night# /rĕally# your /children hòwl every night#	27	13	24	42
64	B3	his /workers entírely distrùsted him# /cĕrtainly# his /workers distrùsted him#	19	12	33	30
67	B4	/Mrs Smith totally rejected his gìft# /hŏnestly# /Mrs Smith rejected his gìft#	14	13	37	22
65	B5	they were /really appalled by their lèader# /frănkly# they were ap/palled by their lèader#	23	9	32	36

Header note: n = 64

Cat no	TEST SENTENCE	n=64 =	?	≠	% 'equals'
60	B6 /frănkly# the /workers were answered by the mànager# the /workers were honestly answered by the mànager#	6	7	51	9
58	B7 /most of them fortunately admired the achìevement# /hăppily# /most of them admired the achìevement#	48	9	7	75
54	B8 /pĕrsonally# I ap/pròved of the idea# /I mysĕlf# ap/pròved of the idea#	58	2	4	91

Table 12

Similarity tests : Battery II

Cat no	TEST SENTENCE	n=179 =	?	≠	% 'equals'
A1	/some people indeed attèmpted it# in/dĕed# /some people attèmpted it#	72	45	62	40
A9	/some lectures are actually given before tèn# /ăctually# /some lectures are given before tèn#	40	39	100	22
A10	the /child surely apologises for his mistàkes# /sŭrely# the /child apologises for his mistàkes#	107	26	46	60
A11	/thĕrefore# /many seats are booked a week befòre# /many seats are therefore booked a week befòre#	156	11	12	87
A12	/sŭddenly# his /friend agrèes to the plan# his /friend suddenly agrèes to the plan#	150	21	8	84
A13	/pĕrsonally# I ap/pròved of the idea# /I pĕrsonally# ap/pròved of the idea#	124	12	43	69
A14	your /father luckily owns a càr# /lŭckily# your /father owns a càr#	88	32	59	49

Table 12 (*continued*)

Cat no	TEST SENTENCE	n = 179			% 'equals'
		=	?	≠	
B9	/rĕally# your /children hòwl during the night# your /children often hòwl during the night#	45	44	90	25
P1	I /don't think he's còming# I /think he's not còming#	99	23	57	55
P3	I /don't know they're stàying# I /know they aren't stàying#	4	17	158	2

Table 13

Similarity tests: Battery III

Cat no	TEST SENTENCE	n = 117			% 'equals'
		=	?	≠	
A15	/lŭckily# the /game ends at sèven# the /game luckily ends at sèven#	77	18	22	66
A16	sur/prĭsingly# your /father owns a càr# your /father surprisingly owns a càr#	72	25	20	62
A17	the /test was surprisingly èasy# sur/prĭsingly# the /test was èasy#	39	23	55	33
A18	the /book was unfortunately dìfficult# un/fŏrtunately# the /book was dìfficult#	29	37	51	25
A19	the /students obviously understood the lècture# /ŏbviously# the /students understood the lècture#	57	31	29	49
A20	the /child understandably feels neglècted# /understăndably# the /child feels neglècted#	96	11	10	82
A21	/wĭsely# the /Minister insisted on a full repòrt# the /Minister wisely insisted on a full repòrt#	104	8	5	89

Table 14

Preference tests : Battery III

Cat no	TEST SENTENCE	+	?	−	1	2	3
		Rating			Ranking		
N7a	Pure and impure love attract the young writer.	82	15	20	76	33	
b	Pure and impure love attracts the young writer.	61	23	33	51	58	
O1a	More than one student attend the lectures.	14	17	86	11	98	
b	More than one student attends the lectures.	106	6	5	105	8	
O2a	Fewer than two students pass the exam.	98	9	10	97	17	
b	Fewer than two students passes the exam.	22	25	70	23	92	
O3a	Each of the children win a prize.	13	18	86	11	100	
b	Each of the children wins a prize.	111	5	1	110	7	
O4a	Of twenty reviewers, each praise my book.	7	22	88	6	103	
b	Of twenty reviewers, each praises my book.	111	5	1	112	3	
O5a	None of the children answer the question.	37	26	54	29	85	
b	None of the children answers the question.	94	10	13	87	26	
O6a	Of thirty critics, none praise your show.	39	30	48	37	79	
b	Of thirty critics, none praises your show.	94	18	5	87	28	
W1a	He need not go.	104	11	2	94	22	
b	He does not need to go.	90	16	11	67	49	
W2a	He doesn't have a car.	75	19	5	40	42	15
b	He hasn't a car. (n = 99)	62	25	12	30	34	33
c	He hasn't got a car.	83	7	9	59	24	14
W3a	He did not dare answer.	82	31	4	53	40	22
b	He dared not answer.	82	28	7	58	36	20
c	He did not dare to answer.	80	23	14	42	39	35
X1a	They have spoiled my holiday.	71	29	17	55	59	
b	They have spoilt my holiday.	85	21	11	77	38	
X2a	His mother spoiled him.	73	30	14	62	51	
b	His mother spoilt him.	78	21	18	65	49	

n = 117

Table 14 (*continued*)

Cat no	TEST SENTENCE	n = 117					
		Rating			*Ranking*		
		+	?	−	1	2	3
X3a	I smelled cabbage.	55	23	39	45	71	
b	I smelt cabbage.	86	18	13	85	29	
X4a	The dinner smelled awful.	58	26	33	42	74	
b	The dinner smelt awful.	88	16	13	83	23	
X5a	I have smelled the flowers.	57	29	31	44	73	
b	I have smelt the flowers.	89	17	11	87	27	•

Table 15

Compliance tests : Battery IV [*cf* Chapter 6]

Test no	TEST SENTENCE	*Task*	RNC *scores* Eng n = 20	Sci n = 20
1	they /used to work here rècently#	S/N¹: *he*	o	o
2	he was /liking beer áll his lìfe#	S/question	8	3
3	a /higher ratio is hard to jùstify#	T/past	o	o
4	his /bathroom was clever to agrèe#	T/negative	5	5
5	the /new rules gave him tròuble#	S/N²: *them*	o	o
6	/every the man day her vìsited#	S/present	4	6
7	he /has a gǐn# but would /rather a whìskey#	T/N¹: *she*	1	2
8	the /dog looks bàrking over ·there#	T/past	3	2
9	there is a /lecture which !I don't know when it will ènd#	S/N²: *he*	4	5
10	/have you bèen there at any tíme#	S/declarat.	16	11
11	/they have done it last wèek#	S/question	16	8
12	he /used to write very long lètters#	T/negative	o	o
13	she /looked at himself by a mìrror#	T/present	4	4
14	/he would have liked to have gòne#	S/N¹: *I*	1	o
15	the /book dispersed alone with the mùsic#	S/question	5	4
16	/patriotism is deficient in yòung people#	T/negative	o	o
17	we /put in the morning the light òff#	T/future	o	o
18	I was /thinking of you last nìght#	S/present	11	6

Test no	TEST SENTENCE	Task	RNC scores Eng n = 20	Sci n = 20
19	he /won't be here a week ago next Jùne#	S/affirmat.	7	3
20	/tea or :còffee [/asked the wàitress#]#	T/future	14	17
21	to /ask me was kìnd of her#	T/negative	0	0
22	I /said that he would gò wóuldn't he#	S/N², N³: *they*	11	11
23	she /used to organise nice pàrties#	S/question	2	1
24	we /showed Mary a pìcture of herself#	S/N²: *Jack*	16	17
25	they a/stonished the new car fòurpence#	T/present	1	2

Table 16

Evaluation tests : Battery IV [*cf* Chapter 6]

Test no	TEST SENTENCE	Eng n = 20 +	−	Sci n = 20 +	−
1	they /used to work here rècently#	12	3	11	2
2	was he /liking beer all his lífe#	3	10	0	8
3	a /higher ratio is hard to jùstify#	20	0	19	0
4	the /barman was never to be sèen#	18	1	18	1
5	the /new rules gave him tròuble#	20	0	20	0
6	/everyone dared her to vìsit it#	14	5	12	3
7	he /has a gĭn# but would /rather a whìskey#	10	1	11	4
8	the /dog looks bàrking over there#	1	17	0	15
9	there is a /lecture which !I don't know when it will ènd#	1	10	1	4
10	you have /bèen there at ·any ·time#	4	7	2	8
11	/have they done it last wéek#	1	11	4	7
12	he /didn't use to write long lètters#	14	2	15	5
13	she /looks at herself by a mìrror#	1	9	3	5
14	he would have /liked to have gòne#	18	0	20	0
15	the /book disappéared# a/long with the mùsic#	16	1	16	0
16	/patriotism is deficient in yòung people#	13	1	17	2

Table 16 (*continued*)

Test no	TEST SENTENCE	Eng n = 20 +	−	Sci n = 20 +	−
17	we /put the light on the lànding off#	10	5	14	1
18	I was /thinking of you last nìght#	20	0	20	0
19	he'll be /here a week ago next Jùne#	1	17	0	18
20	/tea or :còffee [the /waitress will àsk#]#	18	1	14	0
21	to /ask me was kìnd of her#	18	1	16	1
22	I /said that he would gò wóuldn't he#	4	10	1	9
23	did she /use to organise nice párties#	15	0	16	2
24	we /showed Mary a pìcture of him·self#	0	18	0	19
25	the /starfish has a spiny skin for protèction#	19	0	19	1

Table 17

Group results—Compliance and evaluation tests : Battery II

Cat no	Sequence no Order (i)	Sequence no Order (ii)	RNC scores Order (i) groups 1 n=31	2 n=50	3 n=26	RNC scores Order (ii) groups 4 n=17	5 n=21	6 n=34	Evaluation scores Order (i) groups 1 +	1 −	2 +	2 −	3 +	3 −	Order (ii) groups 4 +	4 −	5 +	5 −	6 +	6 −
A1	7	32	5	11	5	3	1	7	1	20	7	30	1	17	1	13	3	13	2	23
A9	11	36	2	10	7	3	0	7	2	21	9	30	2	20	2	11	9	8	6	19
A10	39	15	1	12	6	6	8	13	3	26	4	40	2	21	0	13	1	16	1	29
A11	18	43	3	18	6	5	5	15	2	21	5	34	1	21	0	14	2	13	2	24
A12	28	4	3	19	5	12	14	17	2	24	3	40	2	20	0	15	3	16	3	22
A13	20	45	1	11	4	4	2	8	2	23	6	36	2	19	0	14	3	13	2	26
A14	34	10	1	13	7	5	4	13	1	24	4	37	1	21	1	16	2	16	1	26
B9	32	8	2	5	1	2	0	3	25	2	33	9	20	2	11	1	17	0	25	3
B10	4	29	0	5	0	1	2	1	27	1	44	2	23	1	15	0	17	1	31	2
B11	50	26	0	5	0	3	0	2	26	2	36	6	19	3	10	2	14	2	21	8
C3	9	34	0	5	3	2	0	4	27	2	47	1	25	0	16	0	20	1	31	2
C6	13	38	2	10	7	3	0	7	27	2	44	2	24	1	16	0	19	1	28	1
C9	37	13	2	3	0	0	3	0	26	0	45	3	26	0	13	0	20	0	32	0
C12	44	20	4	12	6	4	5	10	10	14	16	19	11	8	6	4	6	9	4	15
F5	33	9	23	45	22	12	18	28	4	18	11	27	4	13	4	9	2	15	6	19

Table 17 (continued)

Cat no	Sequence no Order (i)	(ii)	RNC scores Order (i) groups 1 (n=31)	2 (n=50)	3 (n=26)	Order (ii) groups 4 (n=17)	5 (n=21)	6 (n=34)	Evaluation scores Order (i) groups 1 +	1 −	2 +	2 −	3 +	3 −	Order (ii) groups 4 +	4 −	5 +	5 −	6 +	6 −
F6	17	42	23	42	21	11	14	26	1	22	8	31	1	19	4	8	0	15	4	25
F7i	3	3	29	43	25	15	19	25	2	15	8	22	4	14	3	10	1	16	6	19
F7ii	51	51	22	36	23	11	15	25	5	17	14	24	9	11	6	5	6	12	8	17
F8	38	14	8	6	6	5	1	10	27	0	49	0	24	0	16	1	21	0	25	4
F9	14	39	2	10	5	2	4	13	30	0	50	0	26	0	17	0	21	0	32	1
H2	2	28	8	13	8	6	5	9	27	1	48	0	25	1	17	0	20	1	30	1
H3	26	1							24	3	34	10	19	4	15	0	15	4	29	2
H6	29	5	14	38	18	9	11	20	2	24	1	39	2	19	0	13	1	16	4	21
H10	36	12	9	22	13	4	6	10	16	6	36	6	15	1	12	2	7	5	22	7
H11	8	33	6	17	11	2	4	9	15	4	31	6	15	5	9	1	14	3	24	8
H12	19	44	8	9	10	2	6	10	18	2	30	8	20	1	14	1	13	2	25	4
H13	45	21	2	9	9	3	1	7	23	2	31	10	16	4	14	0	13	4	26	4
J1	49	25	2	8	5	4	3	7	23	3	42	3	18	4	12	1	15	3	22	5
J2	10	35							28	2	43	4	23	1	16	1	20	1	28	3
J3	23	48	1	5	3	2	2	3	26	2	45	2	23	2	16	1	20	1	29	3
J4	42	18							25	3	36	10	22	2	15	1	16	3	18	7
K1	24	49	2	6	3	3	2	7	16	9	40	6	23	3	13	3	13	6	16	13
K2	46	22	0	0	0	0	1	1	27	1	41	6	24	1	14	1	20	0	25	2

	C1	C2	C3	C4	C5	C6	C7	C8	C9	C10	C11	C12	C13	C14	C15	C16	C17	C18	C19	C20
L₁	21	8	13	7	7	7	9	14	13	29	18	12	12	3	2	7	5	5	35	11
L₂	24	3	10	7	6	5	11	11	15	20	14	8	10	4	2	2	2	2	5	30
M₁	4	27	0	21	0	17	0	26	0	48	1	26	5	0	1	2	7	2	16	41
M₂	15	12	4	13	0	15	5	16	8	36	13	15	11	8	4	9	9	7	25	50
M₃	8	21	2	18	1	15	1	22	3	43	4	24	10	6	5	4	6	3	31	7
M₄	4	26	0	19	0	16	2	23	3	42	2	26	3	0	3	1	6	0	43	19
N₁	31	2	17	3	15	1	26	0	46	2	31	0							1	27
N₂	9	18	6	12	7	8	15	7	25	16	21	7							30	6
P₁	4	30	0	21	0	17	0	26	0	50	0	31	0	0	0	1	2	2	12	37
P₂	1	33	1	20	0	16	0	24	0	50	0	28							41	17
P₃	1	32	0	20	0	16	0	26	0	49	0	30	0	0	0	1	1	0	22	47
P₄	13	14	4	13	8	8	6	11	18	21	12	11	33	17	16	23	49	25	48	24
Q₁	5	26	0	20	1	11	5	18	6	34	3	23	34	20	17	26	50	30	15	40
Q₂	7	23	4	11	6	4	6	7	17	22	11	14	8	4	6	8	21	8	40	16
R₁	6	23	2	18	2	13	7	15	19	24	9	15			6	6	16	2	27	2
R₂	8	23	3	17	1	14	0	24	3	43	5	24	1	1					6	31
R₃	1	31	0	19	0	15	1	24	1	47	1	27							47	23
R₄	5	24	3	18	4	12	2	22	3	47	5	24							21	46

Table 18
Group results—Compliance and evaluation tests : Battery III

Cat no	RNC scores Sequence no Order (i)	(ii)	RNC Order (i) groups D (n=33)	E (n=22)	RNC Order (ii) groups C (n=26)	B (n=18)	A (n=18)	Eval Sequence no Order (i)	(ii)	Eval Order (i) groups D +	D −	E +	E −	Eval Order (ii) groups C +	C −	B +	B −	A +	A −
A15	4	22	28	14	8	5	2	4	13	1	27	3	15	1	21	2	13	1	16
A16	32	44	8	3	5	5	1	21	28	1	27	0	19	1	21	1	15	0	16
B12	11	15	0	0	0	1	0	8	9	30	0	20	2	26	0	16	0	18	0
B13	37	39	0	0	2	4	0	25	24	30	0	20	0	21	1	18	0	17	0
D1	1	25	16	10	19	12	8	1	16	13	13	8	8	15	2	10	1	12	1
D2	12	14	20	13	20	8	8	9	8	11	15	8	8	11	6	8	1	10	4
D3	31	45	22	17	21	16	13	20	29	3	17	3	12	3	12	5	3	2	9
D4	18	8	12	6	8	5	3	12	5	16	6	11	5	10	6	6	4	9	3
D5	38	38	25	17	20	15	12	26	23	0	24	0	20	1	12	1	7	4	7
D6	43	33	27	20	22	17	14	31	28	0	22	0	19	0	16	2	11	2	10
F10	13	13	28	14	17	11	11	10	7	2	20	2	16	1	23	2	13	0	16
F11	45	31	22	14	14	10	10												
F12	39	37	24	11	15	11	9	27	22	17	7	14	5	16	4	13	2	10	3
G1	25	1	1	2	0	1	3	17	32	30	0	20	1	24	1	18	0	18	0
G2	36	40	0	0	0	0	0	24	25	22	8	14	5	16	4	10	5	11	4
G3	47	29	10	10	9	13	6	30	19	5	17	3	18	5	17	5	12	3	11

G4	17	9	14	7	2	2	2	11	6	4	19	5	9	11	7	9	7	10	3
H8	9	17	20	10	14	10	9	6	11	7	12	5	12	8	10	6	8	5	10
H11	33	43	9	6	7	5	0	22	27	16	7	10	6	13	4	9	3	9	4
I1	7	19	0	0	1	0	1												
I2	41	35	0	0	0	1	1												
L3	21	5	2	5	0	0	0	15	2	14	15	7	11	15	7	12	4	8	5
N3								29	20	8	15	7	10	8	12	4	12	6	4
N4								13	4	12	9	8	4	12	5	9	4	7	5
N5								2	15	21	6	6	7	17	2	9	5	13	2
N6								19	30	10	12	7	8	9	4	8	4	8	3
S1	10	16	3	0	1	0	0	7	10	29	2	21	0	17	3	13	4	13	2
T1	29	47	0	0	0	0	0	18	31	27	3	19	0	25	0	18	0	18	0
T2								28	21	31	0	21	1	26	0	16	2	18	0
U1	8	18	2	2	1	4	0	5	12	21	6	19	1	20	0	14	0	15	1
U2	34	42	18	14	22	11	10	23	26	6	14	4	7	11	3	6	4	6	4
V1	20	6	0	0	2	0	0	14	3	31	1	20	0	21	1	14	1	18	0
V2	48	28	15	12	12	6	5	32	17	16	8	11	6	9	5	4	10	9	2
Y1	22	4	25	17	23	17	16	16	1	13	12	8	9	7	6	11	6	5	7
Z1	3	23	9	11	7	7	2	3	14	9	16	2	16	10	10	7	9	10	5

Table 19

Group results—Similarity tests: Battery II

Cat no	Sequence no Order (i)	(ii)	Order (i) 1 n=31 =	≠	2 n=50 =	≠	3 n=26 =	≠	Order (ii) 4 n=17 =	≠	5 n=21 =	≠	6 n=34 =	≠
A1	61	56	9	13	25	15	8	8	10	3	10	8	10	15
A9	53	58	10	15	13	28	3	17	5	6	1	13	8	21
A10	56	61	20	9	26	17	17	6	11	4	14	3	19	7
A11	57	52	28	2	45	4	21	1	14	1	21	0	27	4
A12	55	60	28	0	42	1	21	2	14	0	20	0	25	5
A13	52	57	24	7	35	14	12	11	14	1	15	4	24	6
A14	58	53	13	12	27	17	13	7	5	7	12	5	18	11
B9	60	55	10	15	12	31	2	14	9	5	3	10	9	15
P1	54	59	22	6	29	16	12	11	8	4	8	9	20	11
P3	59	54	0	26	3	45	1	24	0	15	0	20	0	28

Table 20

Group results—Similarity tests: Battery III

Cat no	Sequence no Order (i)	(ii)	Order (i) D n=33 =	≠	E n=22 =	≠	Order (ii) C n=26 =	≠	B n=18 =	≠	A n=18 =	≠
A15	33	39	22	5	13	5	17	4	11	7	14	1
A16	34	38	23	6	16	2	12	5	11	3	10	4
A17	39	33	6	19	4	13	13	11	7	7	9	5
A18	35	37	9	15	5	9	5	12	6	5	4	10
A19	36	36	14	12	11	3	16	5	9	4	7	5
A20	37	35	26	2	16	3	21	3	16	1	17	1
A21	38	34	27	3	18	1	25	0	17	1	17	0

Table 21

Group results—Selection tests : Battery II

Cat no	Sequence no Order (i)	(ii)		Order (i) 1 n=31	2 n=50	3 n=26	Order (ii) 4 n=17	5 n=21	6 n=34
N1	1	27	sg	0	0	0	0	0	0
			pl	31	42	25	6	10	27
N2	30	6	sg	3	2	6	2	4	3
			pl	24	22	20	13	11	23
P1	12	37	V^1	28	37	19	15	19	28
			V^2	3	5	4	2	1	3
P3	22	47	V^1	15	27	16	14	11	25
			V^2	15	18	8	1	9	9

Selected form heading spans Order (i) and Order (ii).

Table 22

Group results—Selection tests : Battery III

Cat no	Sequence no Order (i)	(ii)		Order (i) D n=33	E n=22	Order (ii) C n=26	B n=18	A n=18
N3	46	30	sg	10	4	7	5	6
			pl	23	17	17	10	10
N4	19	7	sg	17	9	13	13	14
			pl	3	3	2	1	3
N5	2	24	sg	27	18	22	10	16
			pl	2	1	4	7	2
N6	30	46	sg	25	18	16	12	17
			pl	7	4	7	3	1
N7	49	27	sg	10	2	14	10	9
			pl	22	19	11	8	9
O1	5	21	sg	30	20	23	16	15
			pl	3	2	2	2	3
O2	14	12	sg	3	2	1	0	1
			pl	29	19	22	18	16
O3	23	3	sg	30	20	23	13	14
			pl	3	1	2	5	4
O4	35	41	sg	29	22	23	15	14
			pl	3	0	1	2	4

Selected form heading spans Order (i) and Order (ii).

Table 22 (*continued*)

Cat no	Sequence no Order			Selected form				
	(i)	(ii)		Order (i)		Order (ii)		
				D $n=33$	E $n=22$	C $n=26$	B $n=18$	A $n=18$
O5	40	36	sg	20	16	11	9	8
			pl	13	5	15	8	10
O6	26	50	sg	16	16	19	12	10
			pl	16	5	6	6	7
X1	24	2	-ed	13	7	11	9	13
			-t	20	15	14	9	4
X2	44	32	-ed	17	11	10	4	10
			-t	14	10	13	14	8
X3	16	10	-ed	10	7	6	6	8
			-t	23	14	19	12	10
X4	27	49	-ed	12	7	7	5	10
			-t	21	15	19	13	7
X5	50	26	-ed	14	8	10	6	8
			-t	18	14	16	12	9

Table 23
Group results—Preference tests : Battery III

Cat no	Sequence no Order (i)	Sequence no Order (ii)	Rating Order (i) D (n=33) +	−	E (n=22) +	−	Rating Order (ii) C (n=26) +	−	B (n=18) +	−	A (n=18) +	−	Ranking ('First' only) Order (i) D	E	Order (ii) C	B	A
N7a	46	41	22	6	18	2	17	5	13	5	12	2	21	18	13	13	11
b			16	6	9	9	16	4	12	6	8	8	15	8	11	8	9
O1a	40	47	4	25	1	18	4	17	2	13	3	13	5	0	3	1	2
b			29	1	20	1	25	0	16	1	16	2	28	21	24	16	16
O2a	49	53	27	4	19	2	22	1	15	1	15	2	27	19	22	16	13
b			8	19	3	16	5	13	3	11	3	11	7	4	5	4	3
O3a	42	45	1	27	3	18	3	17	3	13	3	11	1	2	2	3	3
b			32	0	20	0	25	1	17	0	17	0	32	20	25	16	17
O4a	44	43	1	26	0	20	1	18	1	12	4	12	2	0	2	0	2
b			31	0	21	0	25	0	17	0	17	1	32	22	25	17	16
O5a	51	51	9	16	3	15	11	9	5	9	9	5	8	3	9	4	5
b			26	5	19	0	18	5	16	1	15	2	24	19	18	13	13
O6a	53	49	12	11	5	13	9	9	5	7	8	8	12	4	8	5	8
b			25	1	20	1	20	1	15	1	14	1	23	20	19	15	10
W1a	45	42	29	1	19	1	22	0	18	0	16	0	29	17	18	17	13
b			26	2	19	1	16	4	15	2	14	2	22	16	10	10	9

Table 23 (continued)

Rating columns grouped under Order (i) [D, E] and Order (ii) [C, B, A], with + and − sub-columns. Ranking ('First' only) grouped under Order (i) [D, E] and Order (ii) [C, B, A].

Cat no	Seq no Order (i)	Seq no Order (ii)	D n=33 +	D −	E n=22 +	E −	C n=26 +	C −	B n=18 +	B −	A n=18 +	A −	Rank D	Rank E	Rank C	Rank B	Rank A
W2a	48	54	23	2	15	1	21	2	16	0			15	7	8	10	5
b			20	4	12	5	18	1	12	2			13	5	7	5	10
c			28	2	20	1	20	3	15	3			20	15	15	9	4
W3a	52	50	23	1	19	1	15	1	10	1	15	0	17	13	12	6	10
b			23	2	14	2	14	1	18	0	13	2	16	10	10	12	10
c			18	4	17	4	19	3	13	2	13	1	8	14	10	6	4
X1a	43	44	20	5	10	6	16	3	12	1	13	2	18	10	9	8	10
b			20	3	17	2	21	1	14	4	13	1	20	16	19	12	10
X2a	47	40	20	3	14	4	16	3	11	4	12	0	17	14	11	9	11
b			21	5	14	6	18	1	12	2	13	4	20	11	16	9	9
X3a	41	46	14	9	9	9	12	10	9	8	11	3	14	8	7	6	10
b			24	3	15	3	20	2	14	2	13	3	25	16	20	13	11
X4a	50	52	18	6	7	8	11	10	10	5	12	4	13	6	5	7	11
b			23	4	17	3	22	1	15	1	11	4	23	17	21	13	9
X5a	54	48	16	7	4	12	14	5	11	5	11	2	13	6	7	6	12
b			24	3	19	1	19	3	15	1	12	3	24	18	20	15	10

Bibliographical references

CRYSTAL, D. and QUIRK, R. (1964), *Systems of Prosodic and Paralinguistic Features in English*. The Hague

DAVY, D. and QUIRK, R. (1969), 'An Acceptability Experiment with Spoken Output', *Journal of Linguistics* 5, 109–120

GREENBAUM, S. (1969a), *Studies in English Adverbial Usage*. London

GREENBAUM, S. (1969b), 'The Question of *But*', *Folia Linguistica* III, 3/4

GREENBAUM, S. (1970), *Verb-Intensifier Collocations in English: An Experimental Approach*. The Hague

JACOBSON, S. (1964), *Adverbial Positions in English*. Stockholm

KEMPSON, R. M. and QUIRK, R. (1970), 'Controlled Activation of Latent Contrast by Forced-Choice Selection Tests', (mimeo)

LEECH, G. N. (1969), *Towards a Semantic Description of English*. London

LYONS, J. (1968), *Introduction to Theoretical Linguistics*. Cambridge

MILLER, G. A. and MCKEAN, K. O. (1964), 'A Chronometric Study of Some Relations between Sentences', *Quarterly Journal of Experimental Psychology* 16, 297–308

QUIRK, R. (1970a), 'Taking a Deep Smell', *Journal of Linguistics* 6

QUIRK, R. (1970b), 'Aspect and Variant Inflexion in English Verbs', *Language* 46

QUIRK, R. and SVARTVIK, J. (1966), *Investigating Linguistic Acceptability*. The Hague

SVARTVIK, J. (1968), 'Plotting Divided Usage with *Dare* and *Need*', *Studia Neophilologica* 40, 130–140

TOTTIE, G. (forthcoming), 'Acceptability and Informant Testing', *Moderna Språk*